Lace Lust & LIES

Our shameful affair with the Porn Industry

by Aaron D. Jones

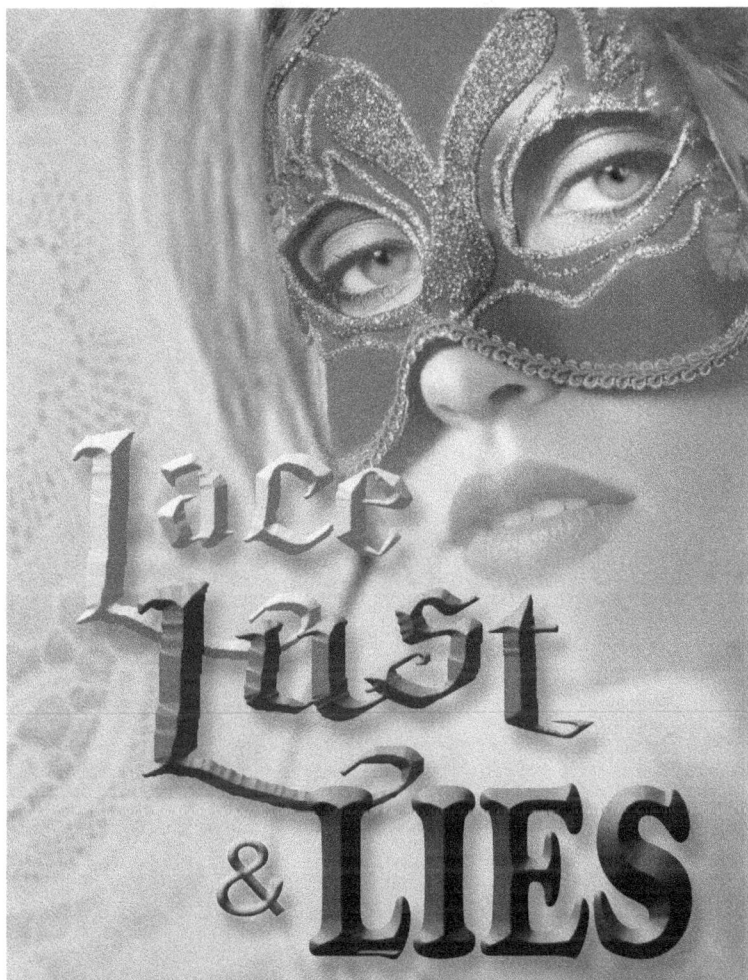

Lace Lust & LIES

Our shameful affair with the Porn Industry

by Aaron Jones

A BOLD TRUTH Publication
Christian Literature & Artwork

"But I say unto you,
That whosoever looketh on a woman to lust after her
hath committed adultery with her already in his heart."

- Jesus Christ
The Son of God, The Word *(A.D. 29 - A.D. 33)*
As recorded in The Gospel of Matthew 5:28

Lace Lust & LIES
Copyright © 2017 Aaron D. Jones
ISBN 13: 978-0-9981531-8-6

Bold Truth Publishing
606 W. 41st, Ste. 4
Sand Springs, Oklahoma 74063
www.BoldTruthPublishing.com
boldtruthbooks@yahoo.com

06 18   10 9 8 7 6 5 4 3 2

Contents

Contents

Foreword

by Michael R. Hicks

The lust of the flesh has been one of the most powerful tools used by Satan and his demonic spirits over the last 6,000 years. The lust for power has imprisoned many in its powerful grip. Even though the lust for power is commanding, the lust for sex is a hundred times worse for just about everyone on earth has been involved at one time or another in various sexual activities.

Lace, lust, and lies are components that are crippling the entire world's moral character. Millions upon millions of people are engaged at this moment in satisfying the flesh, or planning for a chance encounter with someone new to have sex with. People that practice the lust of the flesh are never satisfied nor can they be because it is a never ending quest to enjoy the forbidden fruits of the flesh.

This is nothing new, while Moses went to the mountain to receive the Ten Commandments the people fashioned their gold earrings, bracelets and necklaces into an image of a golden calf. The Bible says, *"They sat down and ate and rose up to play."* This is one of the first recorded orgies in the history of man.

To lust for something is to yearn or to have a strong desire, or to hunger for and to covet the sexuality of others. In today's world, lust is the main instrument for advertising everything from hamburgers; to automobiles; to clothing; to home appliances. The world's focus on lust is so powerful it seems to tap into the lives of every breathing soul.

Aaron Jones' book entitled, "Lace, Lust and Lies" delves into the crippling activities that hinders both men and woman from hav-

Foreword

ing a proper relationship with Jesus. Brother Aaron exposes the deep seeded lust that is hindering men and the Church around the world. He elaborates on the history, the business and the spiritual end of the lust of the flesh and how it affects men and women who are caught in this deadly trap.

In God's sovereignty He has set times for events throughout the history and the future of man. For instance, God declared over three hundred Scriptures about the birth, life and ministry of Christ. So when the fullness of time had come, Jesus was born of a woman and again when the fullness of time came, He died on the cross. Likewise, in the fullness of time when the sins of the people of earth fully reach the nostrils of God, He will send His Son one more time to gather the saints.

Then those who have been practicing the lust of the eyes, lust of the flesh, and the pride of life will suffer badly for the carefree lifestyle they chose to live. There will be millions of men and women who will spend eternity in the flames of fire because they chose a series of sessions of satisfying the lust of the flesh.

We must realize that God will not strive with man forever. We must realize that every sin, every act of disobedience, every act of rebellion, every act on lustful thoughts will bring us closer to the day of the Lord—or Judgment Day.

Acknowledgments

I would like to thank the following people for helping to make this book possible.

To Brian Ohse for the long hours checking, critiquing, and editing this writing. You helped me make the transition from just a bunch of compiled facts and opinions into a flowing marketable book.

Special thanks to 'Chris' for sharing the truth about your personal story of abuse, shame, struggle, and now freedom in Christ. I believe millions will be touched and encouraged by your testimony of Jesus' incredible forgiveness and healing.

To Daryl Holloman and Jim Isreal, my Board Members, intercessors, and trusted Friends. Much appreciation and love to both of you, without your examples of faith, fellowship, input, prayers and support, none of this would be possible.

To Adam, Allen, Christi, Dane, David, Kirk, Nils, Rick, Tallat and Wayne; your never back-down, never stop going for The Gospel, life of Missions continues to make a powerful impact on my life and ministry. You are HEAVENLY LIGHTS SHINING in this world's darkness.

In memory of Rigoberto F. Perez, my good friend and brother in Christ. Thank you for introducing me to Missions and for the work you did around the world for the Kingdom of God. Your ministry herc will never be forgotten and I will see you again.

To Jesus Christ Who rescued me when I was drowning in sin. I had lost everything, and was sure I was not worth saving, but You saved me anyway. I am forever thankful!

Introduction

The New Encyclopedia Britannica[1] states, 'Pornography' is; — representation of sexual behaviour in books, pictures, statues, motion pictures, and other media that is intended to cause sexual excitement.

The word *pornography* comes from the Greek word *porne* meaning "prostituted woman" or "prostitution," and the word *graphos* meaning "writings." Really think about what is depicted in pornography, it is not art, it is not beautiful, nor is it simply sex; it is in reality exactly what the the original Greek *pornographos* was—**"writings or illustrations about prostitutes."**

Mankind already has a problem with lust and ungodly desires. Pornography pours gasoline on what is, in most cases, an already lit fire. We all know what happens when gas is poured on a flame,—WHOOSH! An explosion of heat takes place immediately, often consuming or at the least scorching and damaging everything around it. Get the picture?

> *Proverbs 6:25-28*
> *25. Lust not after her beauty in thine heart; neither let her take thee with her eyelids.*
> *26. For by means of a whorish woman a man is brought to a piece of bread: and the adulteress will hunt for the precious life.*
> *27. Can a man take fire in his bosom, and his clothes not be burned?*
> *28. Can one go upon hot coals, and his feet not be burned?*

It's clear to any discerning eye, the truths in the Scriptures above

---

1 Encyclopedia Britannica

Introduction

can also be applied to a nation as well as an individual. Can you smell the smoke? Verse 26 starts with *"For by means of ..."* or *by this method,* or *this is the way* THE ENEMY USES TO BRING MEN DOWN!

Wake up America!

The Bible gives a stern warning about dabbling with prostitution in any form.

> *Proverbs 23:27 NLT*
> *A prostitute is a dangerous trap; a promiscuous woman is as dangerous as falling into a narrow well.*

The porn industry is simply the commercial sexual exploitation of women on a large scale. The porn industry has done nothing positive, nothing to add to the individual, our families or this nation. It has only advanced the devil's traps and schemes, and in many ways expanded his overall plan to destroy humanity; attempting to move into every aspect of our lives.

As a society, we must recognize the negative and corrosive effects of this industry and turn away from it.

In this book I will give a short summary of the history of pornography: where and how it started, where we are today. Then what the Bible offers those who find themselves trapped in the industry or hooked on its forbidden fruits.

Then when lust hath conceived,
it bringeth forth sin: and sin,
when it is finished, bringeth forth death.
James 1:15

Chapter 1

Heated History

Various depictions (paintings, drawings, carvings, etc...) of nudity are nearly as old as the human race.

UNCOVERING THE ANCIENTS

Discoveries have been made around the world of ancient cave drawings of naked bodies and humans shown in various sexual positions.

For example; in the La Magdelaine Cave in France there is a cave wall engraving, of a reclining female nude, dated back to 15,000-10,000 B.C.[2] This is considered to be one of the first pornographic images on Earth.

One artifact from Egypt, called the Turin Erotic Papyrus has been dubbed the "men's magazine" of its time. It partly consists of explicit depictions of sexual acts and was painted in the Ramesside period (1292-1075 B.C.E.)[3].

---

2   www.ancient-wisdom.co.uk
3   Wikipedia *[History of erotic depictions]*

Old Japanese wood-block printing dating back to 1722 was used to produce and distribute nude images and depictions of sexual activity (it is not known if these were for entertainment or for education).

The Greeks and Romans often painted images of nudity and sex acts on pottery and ceramic tiling.

The peak of erotica for the ancient Chinese was probably around the Ming Dynasty period from 1368–1644 B.C.

In an article by Ilan Ben Zion[4] we find another example of early erotica, i.e., in a Museum display in Israel there are ancient terra cotta plaques from Mesopotamia (dated from the early second millennium), that portray numerous different sexual positions.

India's ancient sex manual the 'Kama Sutra' was written some time between 400 B.C.E and 200 CE.[5]

THE CITY OF SODOM

The Old Testament of The Holy Bible confirms the fact men and women have been interested in each other's bodies since the beginning of time.

In Genesis there is the account of Sodom, a city God destroyed becuase of an overabundance of sin (sexual immorality and homosexuality being specifically mentioned in the text.) Some theologians place this Biblical story back as far as 1700 B.C.

---

4   Ilan Ben Zion, Israel Museum, timesofisrael.com
5   Many historians, e.g., John Keay approximate likely 200 CE.

Genesis 19:5-8
5. *And they called unto Lot, and said unto him, Where are the men which came in to thee this night? bring them out unto us, that we may know them.*
6. *And Lot went out at the door unto them, and shut the door after him,*
7. *And said, I pray you, brethren, do not so wickedly.*
8. *Behold now, I have two daughters which have not known man; let me, I pray you, bring them out unto you, and do ye to them as is good in your eyes: only unto these men do nothing; for therefore came they under the shadow of my roof.*

Genesis 19:24-25
24. *Then the LORD rained upon Sodom and upon Gomorrah brimstone and fire from the LORD out of heaven;*
25. *And he overthrew those cities, and all the plain, and all the inhabitants of the cities, and that which grew upon the ground.*

Then a few days later the Scriptures record a perverted incestuous affair between Lot and his two daughters.

Genesis 19:31-36
31. *And the firstborn said unto the younger, Our father is old, and there is not a man in the earth to come in unto us after the manner of all the earth:*
32. *Come, let us make our father drink wine, and we will lie with him, that we may preserve seed of our father.*
33. *And they made their father drink wine that night: and the firstborn went in, and lay with her father; and he perceived not when she lay down, nor when she arose.*
34. *And it came to pass on the morrow, that the firstborn said*

unto the younger, Behold, I lay yesternight with my father: let us make him drink wine this night also; and go thou in, and lie with him, that we may preserve seed of our father.
35. And they made their father drink wine that night also: and the younger arose, and lay with him; and he perceived not when she lay down, nor when she arose.
36. Thus were both the daughters of Lot with child by their father.

Still to this day, the name 'Sodom' is associated with sin, illicit sex, abominal acts and debauchery.[6] What a sad epitaph on a once great city—left in utter ruin because of sin.

THE MODERN ERA

Most historians agree that what we know as modern pornography, did not start until the Victorian Era.

Looking at that time in history it is obvious the British, French, Italians and Americans have all had their sordid place in the porn timeline. For example; The first known distributed 'nude' painting, was a French impressionist view of a naked prostitute.

According to Wikipedia,[7] "In 1748 the first so-called erotic novel, "Fanny Hill" by John Cleland was published in Great Britain, a book which was later outlawed. The reason; the government charged the author with "corrupting the King's subjects."

When the Italians began excavating the ruins of Pompeii in 1860, they were both shocked and embarrassed by the sheer volume of

---

6   'debauchery' Sodomy [is generally anal or oral sex between people] Wikipedia 1/20/17
7   Wikipedia / https://en.wikipedia.org/w/index.php?title=Fanny_Hill&oldid=771125680

erotic artifacts that had been produced by the Romans and distributed throughout the ancient city.

At the end of the 18th century France was the leading country regarding the spread of porn pictures. Porn[8] became an element of playing-cards, posters, postcards and so on. Today, the porn pictures of that time seem to be rather chaste. But to many people at that time those pictures were scandalous, and public morality campaigns against pornography first began in the 19th century. People caught spreading porn were brought to court and were obliged to pay fines.

MAKING IT ILLEGAL

The English Obscene Publications Act of 1857 made it illegal to distribute these illicit materials. It basically gave the courts the power to confiscate and destroy any offending materials. In London there was an organization called, *"The Society for the Suppression of Vice."*

America soon adopted a similar law into the books; the Comstock Act of 1873.[9]

It was amended in 1876 to prohibit:
[Every obscene, lewd or lascivious book, pamphlet, picture, paper, writing, print, or other publication of an indecent character, ... and every article or thing intended or adapted for any indecent or immoral use, and every written or printed card, circular, book, pamphlet, advertisement or notice of any kind giving information, directly or indirectly, where, or how,

---

8   Pravda.ru *[History of pornography: scandalous beginning and habitual reality]* - 11/27/2007
9   The Accessible Archives; Britannica.com / https://www.britannica.com/event/Comstock-Act / Published: December 01, 1999 - Accessed 04/2016

or of whom, or by what means, any of the before mentioned matters, articles or things may be obtained or made, and every letter upon the envelope of which, or postal card upon which, indecent, lewd, obscene or lascivious delineations, epithets, terms or language may be written or printed, are hereby declared to be non-mailable matter, and shall not be conveyed in the mails, nor delivered from any post office, nor by any letter carriers.] (Comstock, 1967, p. 209).

By 1915 the Author of that Law, Anthony Comstock had some 3,500 people arrested for pornographic related infractions, and him and his team of crusaders had destroyed over 160 tons of what was considered obscene materials.

NOT WORKING

Despite his efforts, the production and distribution of pornography has only grown in the US and around the world.[10]

The fact is: man-made laws and bans are not the whole answer to this problem. These can only deal with vice and lawlessness as society sees it on the surface, but the underlying (unseen) lusts and sinful condition of men's hearts is the real problem.

The most effective way to combat the flow of these materials; is to lead those producing and buying them to a saving relationship with Christ. **Change men's hearts by sharing the Gospel and they will change their habits.**

---

10   pornographyhistory.com and various online information sources / Dec 2015

Thus were they defiled with their own works,
and went a whoring with their own inventions.
Psalms 106:39

CHAPTER 2

Distributing Sin

How did our society come to this place in history where the United States and other western nations now permit depictions of sexual activity that would have been deemed grossly and even criminally pornographic just a few decades ago? It seems in many places the only remaining taboo[11] that is nearly universally recognized is that of child pornography.

For this chapter, we will look mostly at the United States' role in the increase of the porn industry both here and abroad.

TO THE MASSES

By the late 1830's London boasted of more than 50 shops that sold pornographic materials, and by the early 1870's in America, businesses within New York state alone, were selling more than 100,000 porno books per year.

But new ways to exponentially produce and market mankind's

---

11   "taboo" prohibited or restricted by social custom: adj. / Oxford Dictionaries / Yahoo

oldest sins came riding in on the 20th Century's new technology. Better cameras, movie video and high-speed printing presses made it possible to mass market a much higher quality of smut.

ADULT FILMS

Nude photography had been around ever since the invention of a crude form of photo-making called *daguerreotype*, which was invented in the early 1800's.

~

> *Perhaps the filthy image we have really exposed and made public is—*
> *WHAT IS IN MEN'S HEARTS.*

It was the invention of the 'Moving Picture Show' in 1895 that truly caused the porn film industry to take off (no pun intended). Almost immediately after this invention, sex videos began being produced for the public market.

Early pioneers of perversion, Pirou and Kirchner created pornographic films like *"Léar"* and *"Le Coucher de la Marie."* These films opened a wide door for a whole new grade of 'low-class' French films that focused entirely on women undressing, and in many cases parading around in front of the camera nude.

The risqué was not limited to just the French, American men were also intrigued by the prospects of profits being made from something they were already very interested in. Even Thomas Edison's first attempt at moving pictures was of a young woman getting up from a bath and then running away nude.

HARD TRUTH

Just a thought; One would think with all this new copying and imaging technology, mankind would have produced something of more lasting value. Perhaps the filthy image we have really exposed and made public is—WHAT IS IN MEN'S HEARTS.

I am reminded of a couple of Scriptures along this line.

> *Job 5:7*
> *Yet man is born unto trouble, as the sparks fly upward.*

> *Jeremiah 17:9*
> *The heart is deceitful above all things, and desperately wicked: who can know it?*

I know I am not painting a very attractive picture here, but please bear with me, I am wanting to show you where we have come from, in order to have gotten where we are today.

BEGINNING OF BIG MONEY

Then all the lusts and sexual sins got a new big boost; the American Businessman and his insatiable appetite for—the dollar.

U.S. filmmakers saw a giant opportunity in these new naughty movies. American businessmen quickly learned 'Sex sells!" For the United States the slippery slope into the commercial porn industry had already begun.

No longer would the porn industry be only about nudity and sex.

Now it was also about money, and lots of it; as we will see in the next chapter. All those little seeds have grown up into a huge. sick, sin-based billion dollar industry.

> *1 Timothy 6:10*
> *For the love of money is the root of all evil: which while some coveted after, they have erred from the faith, and pierced themselves through with many sorrows.*

At that time some films were being made in Great Britain and the United States, still most of these early dirty videos were produced in France and Latin America. Not to be outdone, the U.S. (mainly Hollywood) would quickly catch up and then **take the perverted lead as the #1 exporter of porn**[12] **in the world.**

SMORGASBORD

Some men were driven by their sexual lusts, and others by their lust for money: either way, Hollywood became a boiling pot of crime, greed, sex, and scandal. Nothing was taboo, if it was marketable, then by all means Hollywood would sell it.

Cheap made 8mm stag films and even cheaper men's magazines became popular in the 1920s. and 30s. Shamefully, the first sexual revolution had hit America.

I heard one man say,
> *"The buffet lines have destroyed America. We are a nation hungry for another plate, more money, more cars, more house, more sex, more entertainment, etc... I need more*

---

12   Google.com, pornographyhistory.com

money, so let's work two or even three jobs, scrape, borrow and steal to get ahead. If this house isn't big enough, we'll build another or buy one bigger. If my wife isn't enough, I'll take another prettier one, younger, sexier, and wilder."

We want, we want, we want for more and more and yet we still remain unsatified.

James 4:2-3
2. Ye lust, and have not: ye kill, and desire to have, and cannot obtain: ye fight and war, yet ye have not, because ye ask not.
3. Ye ask, and receive not, because ye ask amiss, that ye may consume it upon your lusts.

PORN EMPIRES

In 1953 a man named Hefner[13] birthed his own lust-filled vision for the men of America. His men's magazine "Playboy"[14] with it's daring humor, liberal articles and brazen nudity, built an empire by cashing in on men's rebellious spirits and forbidden appetites.

Raunchier magazines like Penthouse[15] and Hustler[16] soon followed, and the American public (mostly men) took the bait.

Penthouse was groundbreaking, in that it showed full frontal nudity and spoke even more frankly about sexual issues.

---

13   Wikipedia contributors. "Hugh Hefner." Wikipedia, The Free Encyclopedia.

14   Playboy -- American monthly magazine for men [The Editors of Encyclopædia Britannica] Encyclopædia Britannica, inc / http://www. britannica.com/topic/Playboy

15   Penthouse men's magazine / owned by Global Media Inc / Wikipedia The Free Encyclopedia / https://en.wikipedia.org/w/index.php?title=Penthouse_(magazine)&oldid=768610036

16   Hustler adult magazine / Wikipedia, The Free Encyclopedia. / https://en.wikipedia.org/w/index.php?title=Pornographic_magazine&oldid=764525911

Still Hustler took adult magazines to a whole new level of erotica and immorality. These magazines and others, were the main source for the public to purchase and view pornography from the early 1900s through the 70s.

A SEX SYMBOL

Having recently posed for a nude photo shoot, Marilyn Monroe was chosen by Hefner to become Playboy's first nude pin-up model. Because she was already a "sex symbol" and a "superstar" in the world's eyes, Marilyn was instrumental in making Playboy Magazine a huge success.

She was so popular, that at one time TV Guide named her, Film's #1 Sexiest Woman of All Time.

But sadly August 5, 1962[17] the world's 'sex symbol" was found dead, nude and face down on her bed with a bottle of pills (barbiturates) supposedly prescribed to help her fight long-term depression.

Sin is very expensive! The old Preachers used to say, *"Sin will take you farther than you want to go, cost you far more than you wanted to pay, and keep you way longer than you wanted to stay."*

NEW TRASH TECH

The entrance of the late 20th century's new video and computer technology caused a significant decline in overall sales of adult printed materials.

---

17   history.com Marilyn Monroe is found dead / http://www.history.com/this-day-in-history/marilyn-monroe-is-found-dead

The 70s had introduced new looser legislation which allowed for another sick monster to rise up. It started in 1957 when the California Supreme Court[18] called a book of poems containing erotic materials; of "redeeming social value" and therefore not classifiable as "obscene." Then later in 1969 a banned Adult Video[19] was declared 'not obscene' by the United States Supreme Court, this opened a wide door of opportunity for other sexually explicit films.

This is not the first time, nor the last time our Supreme Court has made a supreme mistake. Once again they wrongly judged right and wrong by human standards and disregarded God's Word in their decision making process. **Each time this is done the door is opened wider and wider for more evil to come into our nation.**

Isaiah 5:20
Woe unto them that call evil good, and good evil; that put darkness for light, and light for darkness; that put bitter for sweet, and sweet for bitter!

Still other porn producing companies found inroads into the American audience by questionable labeling and shady deals, passing these films off as documentaries or for sex education purposes.

FLOODGATES

Adult theaters and 'private' movie booths in seedy adult bookstores and sex shops seemed to open everywhere almost overnight. These new perverted venues quickly spread across the United States and many other countries like a plague.

---

18   "Roth v. United States." Oyez, https://www.oyez.org/cases/1956/582.
19   "I am Curious (Yellow); Whitebloom, Kenny (10 August 2011). "The Curious Case of 'I am Curious'". Boston TV News Digital Library

To the point that in his 1998 book *"Moral Dilemmas"* by J. Kerby Anderson,[20] he declared adult bookstores out-numbered McDonald's in the United States by a margin of at least three-to-one.

THE BIG SCREEN

Adult films became full-length featured movies in the 70s. What was once hidden in alleys and cheap hotels was now at the local movie theatre. Hollywood studios spewed out movies like:

- Deep Throat (1972)
- Behind the Green Door (1972)
- The Devil in Miss Jones (1973)
- Radley Metzger's The Opening of Misty Beethoven (1975)
- Debbie Does Dallas (1978)

American Cartoonist and Novelist William "Bill" Rotsler[21] made the comment, *"Erotic films are here to stay. Eventually they will simply merge into the mainstream of motion pictures and disappear as a labeled sub-division. Nothing can stop this."*

But much to the surprise of the porn-producers in California, mainstream America didn't buy it. **While Americans want everything exposed to their eyes, evidently they didn't want their nasty desires and lusts exposed to the public eye.** It seems the only sin that trumps lust and sex is—PRIDE.

After all, what would people think if they saw respectable businessmen and women attending such entertainment. Or what would

---

20   "Moral Dilemmas" J. Kerby Anderson (1989)
21   Wikipedia contributors "William Bill Rotsler" The free encyclopedia. Accessed 2016

parents think if they knew where Coach So-in-so and his lovely new wife, the Sunday School teacher spent last Friday night?

I don't know if it is our pride or just fear of men's opinion that makes us protect our public reputation, **and yet at the same time <u>not care</u> what we do in the presence of an all-knowing, holy God?**

> *Hebrews 4:13*
> *Neither is there any creature that is not manifest in his sight: but all things are naked and opened unto the eyes of him with whom we have to do.*

Still the money hungry sex-sellers of Hollywood wouldn't be detoured. The lines of supply and demand had been drawn and crossed—America wanted porn and studios wanted their money.

VHS TAPES

With the invention of the VHS tape and recorder individuals could take porn home with them. This effectively moved dirty movies out of the public theatres; but that was not necessarily a plus.

⌇

"Sin will take you farther than you want to go, cost you far more than you wanted to pay, and keep you way longer than you wanted to stay."

Now more individuals, couples and unfortunately children were exposed to soft and hardcore pornography in their own home, who would have never been exposed to it before.

Even more impacting was the invention of the portable VHS camcorder which made private amateur filming possible. Now anyone who had a camera could make their own dirty movie, either for private or public use.

And to top it all off, in a landmark twisted case "California vs. Freeman"[22] the California Supreme Court basically legalized hardcore pornography.

> *Psalms 53:3*
> *Every one of them is gone back: they are altogether become filthy; there is none that doeth good, no, not one.*

Think about this, according to Covenant Eyes[23] in 2002 alone, there were 11,300 mainstream hardcore films released. There is little doubt that **Jesus knew what He was talking about when He said the world's works are evil.**

> *John 7:7b*
> *... because I testify of it, that the works thereof are evil.*

A TSUNAMI IS COMING

Still, for all the magazines, books and videos the world had only seen the tide come in, and while some large breakers of smut had hit our shores in the past, the big filthy wave of sin was still a little ways out to sea. But it was heading rapidly in our direction, and unfortunately this new wave would become a huge society changing sin-laden tsunami.

---

22   "California vs. Freeman": [The revenge of the Magic Camera] theintenttoarouse.com
23   "© 2015 Covenant Eyes. All rights reserved. Originally published at CovenantEyes.com."

Who knowing the judgment of God, that they which
commit such things are worthy of death, not only do the
same, but have pleasure in them that do them.
Romans 1:32

Chapter 3

Triple XXX at Home

We all soon found out the tsunami of lust and sex had a name, **The World Wide Web - The Internet.** When the late 80's hit, so did a massive wave of filth filled websites.

Almost immediately porn sites took the lead as the #1 use of the Internet. Only until recently pornography related sites and searches have dominated the web. Thankfully that has recently changed. According to *dailyinfographic.com*[24] social media has finally knocked porn off the electronic media mountain.

HOW MUCH MONEY?

Stats from *familysafemedia.com*,[25] released in 2006 show the porn industry had **worldwide internet revenues of $97.6 BILLION.** Think about it, this is only for porn profits on the internet, this does not include DVD or video sales, or other ways pornography is available to viewers.

---

24   "The Stats on Internet Pornography" by Tim (2013) dailyinfographic.com
25   http://www.familysafemedia.com

To put this number into perspective, this revenue is higher than the combined revenue of the top technology companies[26] (Microsoft, Google, Amazon, eBay, Yahoo!, Apple, Netflix and EarthLink).

~

"Sin is very expensive!"

Try to imagine how much impact this is making in the market place, the United States' annual porn revenue exceeds the combined revenues of ABC, CBS, and NBC.

STATISTICS

The following are current estimates[27] based on *dailyinfographic. com's* Jan 2013 Statistics and past rate of growth records.

> ► Every second almost 30,000 people are viewing porn online
> ► Every second over $3,000.00 is being spent on porn and sex related products.
> ► Some 12% of all websites are considered to be pornographic; that's near 25 MILLION sites!
> ► On average 70% of men between the ages of 18-24 visit a porn site every month.
> ► 40 MILLION Ameicans look at porn regularly (1 in 3 are women)
> ► The UK porn industry is estimated to be now worth about 1-billion pounds.
> ► British Web-surfers look up the word "porn" more than anyone in the English-speaking world.[28]

---

26 familysafemedia.com
27 "The Numbers Behind Pornography" by Stewart Cowan (2013) dailyinfographic.com
28 (Lifestyle Trends) / chinadaily.com

► 25% of all search engine requests and 35% of all downloads contain some sort of pornography
► Almost 2.5 BILLION emails daily are pornographic; that's about 8% of all emails
► There are over 116,000 searches for *'child porn'* everyday
► 20% of men and 13% of women admit to having viewed pornography at work

Are you awake yet? You should be!

IN THE CHURCH

While most Christians have hid themselves in their comfortable *'my four and no more'* attitudes and refused to speak out on such base activity. These sins have quietly crept into our churches.

► 47% of Christians surveyed,[29] said porn was a problem in their home.
► 54% of Pastors say they have viewed pornography within the last year
► 50% of Christian men admit they have viewed porn recently
► 37% of these say they are addicted to it
► 20% of Christian women view porn on a regular basis
► Some 56% of all divorces within the Church are blamed on one partner or the other's addiction to pornography.

Charles Swindoll[30] said, *"It is the #1 problem in churches today."*

These facts are staggering! Even alarming when one considers

---

29   dailyinfographic.com, crosswalk.com
30   CP Living at Christianpost.com

again James' words of warning about this very thing,

James 1:15
Then when lust hath conceived, it bringeth forth sin: and sin, when it is finished, bringeth forth death.

Notice he did not say it might bring forth sin, he said it would bring forth sin. **Then once the sin has been done, death comes not far behind.**

A WARNING

Consider The Apostle Paul's words to the Church at Corinth about not lusting and having sexual relations outside of marriage.

1 Corinthians 10:5-8
5. But with many of them God was not well pleased: for they were overthrown in the wilderness.
6. Now these things were our examples, to the intent we should not lust after evil things, as they also lusted.
7. Neither be ye idolaters, as were some of them; as it is written, The people sat down to eat and drink, and rose up to play.
8. Neither let us commit fornication, as some of them committed, and fell in one day three and twenty thousand.

IN THE PRIVACY OF MY HOME

There are over 68 MILLION search engine requests per day for porn! That's 68 MILLION people making a conscious decision and action to sin (sexual sin) EVERYDAY!

Some say there is no harm done. That viewing these things in private is okay, what they do in their own home on their own computer is their business.

But let me repeat again what the writer of Hebrews told us,

> *Hebrews 4:13*
> *Neither is there any creature that is not manifest in his sight: but all things are naked and opened unto the eyes of him with whom we have to do.*

God sees our activity, He knows what is in our heart and He is not pleased. Especially when through the Apostle Paul writing to the Church at Ephesus—GOD TOLD US,

> *Ephesians 5:11-12*
> *11. And have no fellowship with the unfruitful works of darkness, but rather reprove them.*
> *12. For it is a shame even to speak of those things which are done of them in secret.*

WHAT HARM?

We must consider the Old Testament account of Achan and the children of Israel.

God had told Israel, when you take Jericho, don't touch their possessions. He said the city is cursed, and other than putting the gold into the tabernacle treasury, nothing else was to be taken into any one individual's possession.

> *Joshua 6:17-19*
> *17. And the city shall be accursed, even it, and all that are*

therein, to the LORD: only Rahab the harlot shall live, she and all that are with her in the house, because she hid the messengers that we sent.

18. And ye, in any wise keep yourselves from the accursed thing, lest ye make yourselves accursed, when ye take of the accursed thing, and make the camp of Israel a curse, and trouble it.

19. But all the silver, and gold, and vessels of brass and iron, are consecrated unto the LORD: they shall come into the treasury of the LORD.

But there was a man named Achan, that during the battle saw some things he wanted for himself; he lusted after them. He took them and hid them in [the privacy of] his own tent.

A WORD

It would do us good to remember something God spoke to me some time ago in prayer. I heard the Spirit of God say, ***"Not everything set before you, is for you."***

POISON

So too, Achan's sin immediately began to affect Israel's entire camp. In their very next battle, the men of Israel were defeated, thirty-six of them were killed.

When Joshua went to complain before God about their loss, God told him why it happened.

Joshua 7:11
Israel hath sinned, and they have also transgressed my cov-

enant which I commanded them: for they have even taken of the accursed thing, and have also stolen, and dissembled also, and they have put it even among their own stuff.

...and goes on to say.

Joshua 7:12
Therefore the children of Israel could not stand before their enemies, but turned their backs before their enemies, because they were accursed: neither will I be with you any more, except ye destroy the accursed from among you.

ALWAYS REMEMBER

Achan's private lust and sin that HE BURIED IN HIS OWN TENT had affected an army, it had hurt an entire nation. **Poison taken internally will kill your entire body!**

Numbers 32:23
But if ye will not do so, behold, ye have sinned against the LORD: and be sure your sin will find you out.

~

I heard the Spirit of God say, "Not everything set before you, is for you."

SIN AND DEATH

Let me remind you again of this solemn warning.

James 1:15b
... and sin, when it is finished, bringeth forth death.

Payday for these antics is coming! I'm telling you as a watchman[31] called and set up on the wall—PAYDAY IS COMING!!!

It makes no difference who you are, God's stern warning remains.

Romans 6:23a
For the wages of sin is death...

HOW A TSUNAMI BUILDS

Earlier I compared this deluge of lust, sin, sex and filth that is coming on this old world to a *tsunami*. Why?

What happens in a tsunami? Let's look at the makeup and workings of a tsunami.

A tsunami is caused by an earthquake or other disturbance under the ocean surface. This disturbance sends a shock or wave outward in every direction.

Then as the wave approaches land it rises, getting bigger and bigger as the ground rises out of the sea. The problem is, that at a certain height, the wave is forced to collapse down onto everything below it.

The same thing happens with sin, especially when we are looking at the corporate sins of an entire nation. Just take the sin, the population of a nation, and the statistics of supply and demand for

---

31   Ezekiel 3:17, 33:7

porn, and you will see a extremely large wave looming overhead.

It will collapse, and when it does, the sheer weight of the guilt, shame, condemnation and judgement in the wave will crush all that are under it.

THE RIPPLE EFFECT

Comparing these facts to spiritual things, every person overtaken by sin, has first had a disturbance or been shaken under the surface. Evidence or the waves of that disturbance will always surface and expand outward.

Like the ripple of small waves caused by a stone thrown into a pond, or the larger shockwaves created by a suboceanic quake, **sin's affect on an individual cannot be hidden. It will surface! One may hide it for a while, but it will come out.**[32]

> *Mark 4:22*
> *For there is nothing hid, which shall not be manifested; neither was any thing kept secret, but that it should come abroad.*

When there is seismic activity below the ocean's surface, the shockwave of that activity goes to the surface and outward. At first it may be inperceptible to the naked eye, the surface water may not seem to even move at all.

But as it moves away from the epicenter the wave builds as it speeds out in every direction. By the time it hits land, it is a major destructive force and does much damage to established

---

32   Numbers 32:23

structures, often taking millions in both property and lives.

SIN'S FLOOD OF DESTRUCTION

People think: We are watching in the privacy of our own home... so no harm done. But the wave was started, and it built faster and bigger into lives as it raced toward established structures. Foundational structures like the Church and Families.

Now we see divorce at an all time high, one out of every two marriages in North America ends in divorce. That's if they get married at all! More couples are just living together than ever before. Since 2000 we have seen more and more clergy fall victim to sexual sins.

~

Poison taken internally will kill your entire body!

Homosexuality is now considered normal in most U.S. cities. Gay and Lesbian activists are taking advantage of a nation's lust-drunken stupor and have made tremendous inroads into the business sector, the media and even into our schools.

This nation has fell victim to the old adage: **"If you don't stand for something, you will fall for anything!"**

AFTER ITS OWN KIND

And where we have chosen to not turn off the Television, failed to reject that R-rated movie, or refused to avoid that questionable

Website, the consequences or harvest of those failures now plays out publicly before us daily.

God told Adam and Eve in the garden, *"every seed will produce after its own kind."* In other words, corn will make corn, apples will grow apple trees, etc.

> *Genesis 1:11-12*
> *11. And God said, Let the earth bring forth grass, the herb yielding seed, and the fruit tree yielding fruit after his kind, whose seed is in itself, upon the earth: and it was so.*
> *12. And the earth brought forth grass, and herb yielding seed after his kind, and the tree yielding fruit, whose seed was in itself, after his kind: and God saw that it was good.*

And the scarier part is; like a tree or a row of corn, the crop (harvest) is always far bigger than the seed sown.

Now let me repeat what I stated earlier; **Sin will always take you farther than you intended to go, keep you longer than you had planned to stay and cost you far more than you intended to pay!**

*THE HANDWRITING ON THE WALL

Do not be fooled, for both the individual and as a nation, judgement is coming. Like King Belshazzar[33] of old, we have taken things God meant to be used to represent His covenant in beauty and holiness and threw a drunken party with them.

But just as the fingers of God that wrote divine judgement and

---

33   Then they brought the golden vessels that were taken out of the temple of the house of God... Dan 5:1-5 King James Version / Public Domain

the King's demise on the plaister of the wall. The Bible tells us there is an eternal end rapidly coming upon this generation's sexual escapades. Very, very soon the party will be over!

Galatians 6:7-8a AMP
7. Do not be deceived and deluded and misled; God will not allow Himself to be sneered at (scorned, disdained, or mocked by mere pretensions or professions, or by His precepts being set aside.) [He inevitably deludes himself who attempts to delude God.] For whatever a man sows, that and that only is what he will reap.
8. For he who sows to his own flesh (lower nature, sensuality) will from the flesh reap decay and ruin and destruction...

---

*For an eye-opening read concerning current events and the judgement to come get **"The Handwriting on the Wall"** *a book of Poetic Prophecies* by Marcella O'Banion Burnes.

For he that soweth to his flesh
shall of the flesh reap corruption;
but he that soweth to the Spirit
shall of the Spirit reap life everlasting.
Galatians 6:8

Chapter 4

Bad Seeds

Most have heard somebody describe a more rowdy person's actions or lifestyle by saying, *"They are sowing their wild oats."*

That statement is more accurate than many may realize, for sowing seeds is an activity God originated. From the beginning He set in motion the law of *sowing and reaping*,[34] and it operates perfectly just as God designed it every time and for everything on this planet.

SEEDTIME AND HARVEST

Galatians 6:7
Be not deceived; God is not mocked: for whatsoever a man soweth, that shall he also reap.

Genesis 8:22
While the earth remaineth, seedtime and harvest, and cold and heat, and summer and winter, and day and night shall not cease.

---

34   While the earth remaineth, seedtime and harvest... Genesis 8:22 King James Version / Public Domain

Nothing just happens, there is always cause and effect, *seedtime and harvest.* First a seed is sown, and then later there is a harvest on that seed. Referring to sex; something happens, maybe an image was viewed either in a book or on video, or a molestation happened, etc., then later in life these things manifest as sexual sin.

WAKE UP! We have sowed to the flesh, sowed to the flesh and sowed to the flesh[35] over and over in films, magazines, photos and websites. For years we have planted wicked seeds of lust, fornication, adultery, perversion and even bestiality.

Seemingly no one cared, no one noticed, so no harm done? But that is a LIE! **Unseen does not mean undone!**

The enemy of man's eternal destiny did not bait the trap for nothing: he has not spread his poison throughout the media just to sit down with you for a social visit. **No, no the devil is playing for keeps! You cannot flirt with sin, just sipping the poison is no less dangerous, you are still injesting POISON!**

THE TRAP IS SET

First the mouse sees and smells the cheese (senses aroused), then when no one is looking, attempts to sneak a bite (and may even get away with it once or twice), but eventually the trap bar will spring faster than the mouse can get away, and he will be caught; his life destroyed; **DEAD WHERE HE GAVE IN TO TEMPTATION.**

Romans 6:16
Know ye not, that to whom ye yield yourselves servants to

---

35   For he that soweth to his flesh shall of the flesh reap corruption ... Galatians 6:7-9 King James Version / Public Domain

obey, his servants ye are to whom ye obey; whether of sin unto death, or of obedience unto righteousness?

It is impossible to sow bad seeds and not get a bad harvest. *Seedtime and harvest* <u>is a law</u> that has already been put in place, and it will not be compromised. It will take place!

Someone once said, *"The wheels of justice turn slow, but they do keep turning."*

I will again inject this very important truth from God's Word.

Galatians 6:8
For he that soweth to his flesh shall of the flesh reap corruption; but he that soweth to the Spirit shall of the Spirit reap life everlasting.

I believe the reaping or the harvest is now here! Remember, seeds produce after their own kind. NOTE: Again the above verse says.

...he that soweth to his flesh shall of the flesh reap corruption;

SOWN SEEDS

Let's look at that closer. We've sowed:
- ► Sexual images
- ► Sexual Perversion
- ► Voyerism
- ► Lust
- ► Fornication
- ► Adultery
- ► Child Porn

- ► Molestation
- ► Bestiality
- ► Sodomy
- ► Investing Billions in a dead thing (the Porn Industry)
- ► and more...

REAPING A HARVEST

We are now reaping:
- ► 62,000,000 Aborted Babies
- ► HIV/AIDS
- ► other STDs
- ► High Divorce rate
- ► Lost (younger) generation
- ► Increase of Rape and Violence against women
- ► High rate of Child Abuse
- ► Political correctness and suppression of Biblical Marriage and the True God ordained family unit
- ► Shame
- ► Condemnation
- ► Failing Economies
- ► and more...

Now, I know people may disagree about some of the above harvests being directly connected to the seeds I listed. Yet, sadly it is all still happening and increasing whether we agree or not.

OLD SEEDS

Humans are funny in that we think because things don't happen on our schedule, it's not going to happen. Nothing could be further from the truth. Just as the wheels of justice slowly keep turning. The same is true of the law of 'Seedtime and Harvest.' Just because you have not seen a tree yet, does not mean the seed sown isn't still waiting, germinating, preparing to burst forth from the ground of your life, either as productive fruit or as a destructive weed depending on what has been sown.

~

It is impossible to sow bad seeds and not get a bad harvest. Seedtime and harvest is a law...

Job 14:7-9
7. For there is hope of a tree, if it be cut down, that it will sprout again, and that the tender branch thereof will not cease.
8. Though the root thereof wax old in the earth, and the stock thereof die in the ground;
9. Yet through the scent of water it will bud, and bring forth boughs like a plant.

Many people find themselves in situations and dire circumstances and don't know why. It is because of seeds they have sown somewhere in their past, e.g., that adult magazine he looked at as a teenager was planted in his soul, and now as a married man and father, he finds himself in the destructive harvest of adultery.

THIS IS NO GAME! Again, sin will cost you far more than you ever wanted to pay!

A LITTLE LEAVEN

In his book 'Kingdom of Light II kingdom of Darkness[36] (2017) Author and Minister Michael R Hicks said this,

"An example of this is, when a person looks at a little pornography, he is opening the door for sexual immorality, which is demonic. A little leaven is that first look. When that first look is lingered upon, demonic spirits will begin titillating you to take further action. Imaginations of sexual liaisons will pop-up in your brain like they do on your computer. When your imaginations have run its course, it will bloom into obsessions. This action will lead you into looking for someone to satisfy the lust you have been demonically renewing your mind with. This pushes people to clubs, strip joints, laundry mats, grocery stores, red light districts, and day care centers to satisfy their urge for sexual contact. For some, they will hide in the bushes so that they may jump out and take what they want. Porn (lust of the flesh) has its hooks in so many people that sexual predators are being televised as entertainment. As I stated earlier, sin is very expensive and always takes people further than they planned to go. Small activities will always have the propensity to grow up into huge events."

James 1:14-15
14. But each one is tempted when he is drawn away by his own desires and enticed.
15. Then, when desire has conceived, it gives birth to sin; and sin, when sin is full grown, brings forth death.

---

36 'Kingdom of Light II kingdom of Darkness -- Spiritual Warfare and The Church' by Minister Michael R. Hicks (2017) Used by permission.

THE WHOLE STORY

See the devil doesn't tell you about the consequences, when he offers you that magazine or video. He fails to mention their disease when he introduces you to that hot new girl or good looking guy. There are no warning labels or fine print on most of the packages the world is selling.

You've heard, "You have to pay to play!" Well the other side of that coin is, "You get exactly what you pay for!"

The convicted pedophile never intended to touch a boy or girl when he first started looking at Adult Magazines. But somewhere along the way with the devil's continual influence, he allowed his lusts and restraints to go beyond reasonable lines.

The young woman never thought she would get HIV, when she read that first Adult Romance Novel. He was so handsome, like the fairy-tale prince in the graphic love story she just finished. She thought, just one night together, she could give him her body and he would give her his love; but instead—he gave her a disease.

When we put the wrong fuel into our eyes, ears and minds, then our thoughts paint imaginary pictures of heavenly ecstasy. Unfortunately 99.9% of these illusions when acted out bring us to bondage, problems and torment (emotionally, physically, spiritually, etc...) consequences often painted permanantly on the canvas of our lives.

Romans 6:16 AMP
Do you not know that if you continually surrender yourselves to anyone to do his will, you are the slaves of him whom you obey, whether that be to sin, which leads to death, or to obe-

dience which leads to righteousness (right doing and right standing with God)?

Always remember, the devil is a liar[37] and everything he has ever initiated was a cheap counterfeit, destined for destruction, along with everything and everyone involved in it.

LUST OF THE FLESH

King David fell into the *voyerism* trap, while on his own rooftop one evening.

The Dictionary[38] defines *'voyer'* as; --
1. one obtaining sexual gratification from observing unsuspecting individuals who are partly undressed, naked, or engaged in sexual acts; broadly: one who habitually seeks sexual stimulation by visual means
2. a prying observer usually seeking the sordid or the scandalous

Basically it's pornography in real life, in other words the man or woman being viewed is in front of you, instead of in a magazine or photograph. This was David's downfall.

> *2 Samuel 11:2*
> *And it came to pass in an eveningtide, that David arose from off his bed, and walked upon the roof of the king's house: and from the roof he saw a woman washing herself; and the woman was very beautiful to look upon.*

---

37   ... there is no truth in him (John 8:44) King James Version / Public domain
38   "Voyeur." Merriam-Webster.com. Merriam-Webster, n.d. Web. 7 Jan. 2016.

MODERN REVELATION: - He saw the beautiful model and liked what he saw. He lusted after (wanted her sexually) her physical body. So he watched her washing (bathing, showering; nude or at least partially nude.) He was hooked!

2 Samuel 11:3
And David sent and enquired after the woman. And one said, Is not this Bathsheba, the daughter of Eliam, the wife of Uriah the Hittite?

MODERN REVELATION: - Now he had to see her again, he had to get another copy. He believed seeing her again, would satisfy his male hunger for female companionship. He wanted to somehow paint the picture of the sexual image he had already created in his mind.

2 Samuel 11:4
And David sent messengers, and took her; and she came in unto him, and he lay with her; for she was purified from her uncleanness: and she returned unto her house.

MODERN REVELATION: - He acted on what he had been looking at. The bad seeds of lust he had allowed to enter through his eyes and race through his mind, now manifested in the sexual sin of adultery.

The seeds of lustful thoughts and intentions he had sown, now manifested as a huge crop (harvest) of SIN!

The old saying is true -- **"When you see what you shouldn't see, and go where you shouldn't go. You will end up doing what you shouldn't do!"**

WHAT THE EXPERTS SAY

"Pornography, by its very nature, is an equal opportunity toxin. It damages the viewer, the performer, and the spouses and the children of the viewers and the performers. It is toxic miseducation about sex and relationships. It is more toxic the more you consume, the 'harder' the variety you consume and the younger and more vulnerable the consumer."

- *Dr. Maryanne Layden,[39]
Director of Education,
Center for Cognitive Therapy,
University of Pennsylvania, Philadelphia, P.A.

*Dr. Layden is also the Director, Social Action Committee for Women's Psychological Health, Philadelphia.

■■■■

"Under controlled experimental conditions, massive exposure to pornography resulted in a loss of compassion toward women as rape victims, and toward women in general."[40]

- Dolf Zillmann
Professor
Senior Associate Dean for graduate studies and research
College of Communication and Information Sciences
University of Alabama

■■■■

"After looking at adult porn a long time, they get bored. They want something different. They start looking at chil-

---

39   clinicalcareconsultants.com, by Dr. Maryanne Layden [Pornography Statistics]
40   Paper to the Surgeon General's Workshop on Pornography and Public Health, University of Indiana: -- Alington, Virginia (June 1986)

dren. Then, they can't get enough of it."
> \- David G. Heffler, Psychotherapist
> Counsels child pornography offenders

■■■■

"The findings of numerous studies suggest that pornography consumption promotes sexual deviancy, sexual perpetration, and adverse sexual attitudes."
> \- Dr. James B. Weaver, Professor,
> Virginia Polytechnic,
> Institute and State University,
> Department of Communication, Shanks Hall,
> Blacksburg, VA

■■■■

"When we considered men who were previously determined to be at high risk for sexual aggression... we found that those who are additionally very frequent users of pornography were much more likely to have engaged in sexual aggression than their counterparts who consume pornography less frequently."
> \- Neil Malamuth
> Psychologist
> Professor
> University of California Los Angeles (UCLA)
> Los Angeles, California

■■■■

"In interviews I did with seven incarcerated sex offenders, aged from their late thirties to early sixties, all said that the quality and quantity of their porn use changed drastically after the introduction of the internet... The average length of

time between downloading the first child porn and sexually assaulting a child was one year. Most men told me that before becoming addicted to Internet porn, they had not been sexually interested in children."

- Gail Dines[41]
Author and Activist
Professor of Sociology and Women's Studies
Wheelock College in Boston, Mass.
Anti-pornography Lecturer.

CHILD ABUSE ON THE RISE

In a report by the U.S. Congress Permanent Subcommittee on Investigations on Child Pornography and Pedophilia[42] (1986)

No single characteristic of pedophilia is more pervasive than the obsession with child pornography. The fascination of pedophiles with child pornography and child abuse has been documented in many studies and has been established by hundreds of sexually explicit materials involving children.

Detective Dworin of the Los Angeles Police Dept. estimates that of 700 child molestation arrests he has participated in during the last ten years, more than half had child porn in their possession. About 80 percent owned either child or adult pornography.

Child pornography plays a central role in child molestations by pedophiles, serving to justify their conduct, assist them in seduc-

---

41   (*Described as the world's leading anti-pornography campaigner) from [Pornland: How Porn has Hijacked our Sexuality] 04/26/2011 Beacon Press
42   Paper to the Surgeon General's Workshop on Pornography and Public Health, University of Indiana: -- Alington, Virginia (June 1986)

ing their victims, and provide a means to blackmail[43] the children they have molested in order to prevent exposure.

According to the US Department of Justice "One in three females and one in ten males will be sexually molested before the age of 18. Four million child molesters reside in the United States.[44]

FACT: 82% of boy child molesters studied have admitted to regularly using hard core pornography.

~

See the devil doesn't tell you about the consequences, when he offers... There are no warning labels or fine print on most of the packages the world is selling.

Of the 1400 child sexual molestation cases in Louisville, Kentucky between July 1980 and Febuary 1984,[45] adult pornography was connected with each incident and child pornography with the majority of them.

RAPE STATISTICS[46]

► Around 89,000 rape cases are reported in the US annually
► 16% of women have experienced an attempted or completed rape

---

43   U.S. Congress Permanent Subcommittee on Investigations on Child Pornography and Pedophilia (1986)
44   US Department of Justice [Research on Pornography] documented antisex.com
45   from "Moral Dilemmas" by J. Kerby Anderson (1998)
46   statisticbrain.com [Accessed 2015]

▶ 3% of men experience an attempted or completed rape
▶ Only 40% of rapes are ever reported to authorities
▶ 95% of college rapes are never reported to authorities
▶ In 47% of rapes both victim and perpetrator had been drinking

According to a study done by Michigan State Police (Lt. Darrell H. Pope.[47])

In his study recording the use of pornography in sex crimes. He researched 48,000 sex crimes spanning a 20 year period (1956-1979). (Research was done in 1977, replicated in 1981).

In 42% of the 48,000 sex crimes investigated, police indicated that **pornography was involved** - used just prior to, or during the act of sexual assault - as stated by the victim or the offender.

SEX TRAFFICKING

▶ One of the primary purposes of human trafficking is to compel victims to commit sex acts for creating pornography.
▶ According to some estimates, approximately 80% of trafficking involves sexual exploitation.
▶ The average age a teen enters the sex trade in the U.S. is 12 to 14-year-old. Many victims are runaway girls who were sexually abused as children
▶ California harbors 3 of the FBI's 13 highest child sex trafficking areas in the nation: Los Angeles, San Francisco, and San Diego.[48]

---

47   Lt. Darrell H. Pope [Research on Pornography] - antisex.com
48   dosomething.org

SIN BEGATS MORE SIN

The practices or manifest harvest that result from habitual pornography use, like e.g., fornication *(Acts 15:20, 29)*; adultery *(Lev 18:20)*; bestiality *(18:23)*; homosexuality *(18:22 and 20:13)*; incest *(18:6-18)*; and prostitution *(Deut 23:17-18)* have all already been condemned by the Word of God.

One wouldn't think God would have to mention incest or bestiality? But then sin in its rawest form is abominable, base, nasty and vial. Evidently the flesh of man when serving the wrong master knows no limits in its lust-driven downward spiral.

SCENE OF THE CRIME

Everyone knows The Bible forbids both fornication (sex outside or before marriage) and adultery (sex with some one other than your spouse); but few people know that in many states and towns laws are still on the books that make it illegal to have sex with anyone other than your spouse. So then, two people having 'casual sex' are actually commiting a crime (<u>sin</u>) against themselves, God, the laws of the land, and society.

> *1 Corinthians 6:18 NLT*
> *Run from sexual sin! No other sin so clearly affects the body as this one does. For sexual immorality is a sin against your own body.*

> *Hebrews 13:4 NKJV*
> *Marriage is honorable among all, and the bed undefiled; but fornicators and adulterers God will judge.*

DEAD BABIES TELL NO TALES

According to the Urban Dictionary a 'cleaner' gets rid of evidence like bodies, blood, weapons, fingerprints, and <u>even witnesses in order to hide the proof</u> or notion of the crime.

God showed me that is <u>a perfect description of abortion.</u> Two people commit a sexual crime (sin) and then guilt, shame and condemnation demand they have the only witness killed (removed). Since Roe vs. Wade there have been over **62,000,000— MILLION <u>tiny witnesses</u>** 'cleansed' from our sexual crime scenes. THINK ABOUT THAT!!! Their body, blood, DNA, inherited characteristics—the proof; ALL stripped from the scene before they ever have a chance to point to Momma and Daddy.

THE HIGH COST OF TOMORROW

If this is our harvest so far, try to imagine the horrifying harvest we have coming if we continue down this path of sowing to every fleshly whim and desire!

Luke 13:5
I tell you, Nay: but, except ye repent, ye shall all likewise perish.

Payday is coming! ...and I'm afraid the price for all the evil deeds which have overtaken us will be far too high.

2 Peter 2:14
Having eyes full of adultery, and that cannot cease from sin; beguiling unstable souls: an heart they have exercised with covetous practices; cursed children:

Were they ashamed when they had committed abomination?
nay, they were not at all ashamed,
neither could they blush...
Jeremiah 6:15a

Chapter 5

Not Shocked

People today have been desensitized, clearly we are numb and/
or calloused to everything. In our twenty-first century society
where most everything abnormal is normal—nothing shocks us.
People feel as if they have seen it all, and some of them are right,
they have! Most of us are like a popular modern t-shirt design
says "Been there, done that!"

NUMB

This numbing effect or callousing has not been to our benefit.
We as a people no longer feel, we can't feel the pain of others,
we have no sense of guilt or remorse for our sins or the sins
of others. We are numb to the fact God is not pleased, we've
become hard and calloused to His Word and His leadings. No
longer are we convicted about our sins, sadly we have been desensitized to the point that not only do we not feel condemned,
but we can't see the precarious condition we as individuals and
our society is in.

So consequently Christian things don't affect us as they should; we no longer rejoice over blessings,[49] big or small, neither do we weep over things that should break our hearts. We now have a hard shell over our minds and emotions, and we don't allow too much in.

Like the ancient citizens of Ninevah, we have been domesticated or dumbed down, conditioned by our experiences and surroundings.

> *Jonah 4:11*
> *And should not I spare Nineveh, that great city, wherein are more than sixscore thousand persons that cannot discern between their right hand and their left hand; and also much cattle?*

How did this happen?

NON-BLUSHING SAINTS

Again I remind you of our key verse for this chapter.

> *Jeremiah 6:15*
> *Were they ashamed when they had committed abomination? nay, they were not at all ashamed, neither could they blush: therefore they shall fall among them that fall: at the time that I visit them they shall be cast down, saith the LORD.*

The word *'blush'* in the above verse is the Hebrew word[50] (*kä·läm'*) meaning; -- to insult, shame, or humiliate
    a. - blush
    b. - be ashamed, be put to shame
    c. - be reproached

---

49   Romans 12:15 / http://www.BlueLetterBible.org / Accessed 2017.
50   'blush' New Strong's Exhaustive Concordance [by James Strong] May 21, 2003

d. - be put to confusion
e. - be humiliated

The people of that time in Nineveh had become hard, they weren't even ashamed of their ungodly acts. This hardness or callousness caused **their sins to no longer bother them. The fact their actions displeased God simply no longer concerned them.** Their abominable sins didn't even embarass them.

That is exactly the same condition our society (even in The Church) is in today. Sin no longer make us ashamed, nothing embarrasses us. Numb on the inside, we have lost our moral compass, (that right or wrong feeling down inside); we've lost our spiritual senses.

UNCONCERNED

I have watched a change that has taken place over the last few years in this country and in The Church. That change is; **people are no longer concerned about God's view of things.**

This is all part of being numb and calloused. When a hand is severely calloused, it doesn't feel or perceive cold, hot or even pain as readily as a hand that is not calloused.

It is the same with numbing. When a Doctor or Dentist numbs an area of your body, it is to keep you from feeling pain.

The devil has effectively done this to people spiritually. We are numb and hardened to most any stimuli, either good or bad, righteous (holy; inline with God's Word) or unrighteous (unholy; against God's Word).

Matthew 13:15a
For this people's heart is waxed gross, and their ears are dull
of hearing, and their eyes they have closed;...

The word *'gross'* in this verse meaning;[51] - to make stupid (to render the soul dull or callous)

Matthew 24:12
And because iniquity shall abound, the love of many shall
wax cold.

The phrase *'wax cold'* is the Greek word[52] ψύχω (*psü'-khō*) - it's where we get our English word psycho. It means to grow cold, or get cold by being blown on.

Think about it, once again He is referring to people becoming dull, slow, cold, hard, etc...

Church WE MUST WAKE UP!!!

KEEP YOUR HEART

Actually it is quite easy to become hard in this fast paced high-tech enviroment. But all the blame cannot be placed solely on our surroundings, when ultimately the responsibility is on us.

Proverbs 4:23
Keep thy heart with all diligence; for out of it are the issues
of life.

---

51   'gross' New Strong's Exhaustive Concordance [James Strong] May 21, 2003
52   'wax cold' ψύχω (*psü'-khō*) New Strong's Exhaustive Concordance [by James Strong]
May 21, 2003

In this verse the word *'keep'* is the Hebrew word[53] *'natsar'* or (*nä·tsar'*) which means; - guard, preserve, guard from dangers, to be kept close, to be blockaded

However in the day we are living, most believers have failed to do so. In our day most Christians don't guard anything, nor is there any separation! The lines between The Church and the world have been severely blurred, with many reading what the world reads, watching what the world watches and going where the world goes.

∽

> ## *"When you see what you shouldn't see, and go where you shouldn't go. You will do what you shouldn't do!"*

They totally disregard the Biblical admonition to *"Keep thy heart with all diligence."*

TIME AND EXPOSURE

Many Christians are like Lot. With their eyes on their surroundings, many have compromised their position and allowed what they've seen and heard to harden their heart.

2 Peter 2:7-8
7. And delivered just Lot, vexed with the filthy conversation of the wicked:
8. (For that righteous man dwelling among them, in seeing

---

53 'keep' New Strong's Exhaustive Concordance [by James Strong] May 21, 2003

and hearing, vexed his righteous soul from day to day with their unlawful deeds;)

Our steady diet of TV, Radio, Books, Magazines and Internet have desensitized us. Some Christians no longer feel, they don't sense or see those things that affect their lives, either good or bad.

As believers our hearts are supposed to be soft, pliable, gentle and sensitive. But unfortunately that is no longer the case. Like the hands of one doing hard manual labor for years, our hearts have been rubbed, worn and scarred till the emotional surface has hardened and calloused over.

This doesn't happen overnight, just like the worker's hands, people's hearts and minds have been exposed over and over again to sin and the things of this world, until they have become hard.

A FROG'S COMFORT

We all know that if you place a frog in a boiling pot of water, he will immediately respond to the discomfort and explode out of it, thrashing, hopping, and splashing as if he is on fire.

But I have been told, you can take that same frog and place him in a pot of room temperature water and slowly turn up the heat underneath it. By bringing the water temperature up ever so slowly one can supposedly heat it all the way to the boiling point and the dumb frog will never jump out. The frog will actually cook to death and never move. Why?

Because like the numb calloused over Christian, **the frog is comfortable in what he is sitting in.** Oh it's a little warm, but the change came so slowly he never realized <u>how dangerous</u> his position really was.

The little frog started out in the right spot, but things around him heated up. Unaware of the danger, he cooked where he sat.

WAKE-UP CALL

Many people are cooking right where they are! They're no longer embarrassed at dirty jokes or questionable imagery. They no longer shun worldly attractions, or care that it is now at their doorstep. For many, sin is not only at your door but also on your bookshelves, in your closets, on your ipads, phones, computers and televisions.

The enemy of our souls has turned the heat up and many still haven't moved! Hell's fires are cooking many folks right where they sit.

Some in our Churches and even in Ministry have put on life preservers, others are trying to float or tread the heated waters. But sadly, as I said before, <u>many are being cooked right where they are!</u>

I must shout to you—**WAKE UP CHURCH!!!**

Unless people get free of this porn stuff, they are doomed! Christian, never allow yourself to warm up to it, to get comfortable in it. **You must get out now, so JUMP! As a believer one must move quickly up and out of the things this world is offering.**

2 Corinthians 6:15-18
15. And what concord hath Christ with Belial? or what part

hath he that believeth with an infidel?

16. And what agreement hath the temple of God with idols? for ye are the temple of the living God; as God hath said, I will dwell in them, and walk in them; and I will be their God, and they shall be my people.

17. Wherefore come out from among them, and be ye separate, saith the Lord, and touch not the unclean thing; and I will receive you,

18. And will be a Father unto you, and ye shall be my sons and daughters, saith the Lord Almighty.

MEN, THIS IS WAR!

The devil is not playing,[54] **this is not a game!** The things of this world are designed to destroy all who become involved with them. This is an assignment to destroy you and all that you hold dear in this life and beyond. Don't allow yourself to be cohersed, or lured into the devil's snare.[55]

And don't think you are immune, or that you can control yourself under fire (temptation). This is not a new strategy, many a good soldier or leader has been lured into the enemy's camp by a seductive beautiful woman. <u>You must be a disciplined soldier,[56] ever alert to his plans and schemes!</u> All of the enemy forces aren't dressed in military fatigues[57] and armed with rifles, some of his best aren't even on the battlefield; and some of the most dangerous aren't even clothed!

54　the thief cometh but to kill, steal and to destroy. John 10:10 King James Version

55　1 Timothy 3:7; 2 Timothy 2:26 King James Version / Public domain

56　2 Timothy 2:3 King James Version / Public domain

57　...an angel of light 2 Corinthians 11:14 King James Version / Public domain

TEST YOURSELF

Have you become cold-hearted? Are you numb?

Just think about it, test yourself. The next time you walk outside, what would have to happen on the sidewalk for you to be shocked? Not that you may not like it, you might even turn from it, but be real honest with yourself: What would actually shock you?

What would it be?
  – Someone dead?
  – A shooting?
  – A streaker?
  – A couple in a sexual embrace?
  – A man shouting foul language?
  – A naughty poster or billboard?
  – A riot?

Do you see my point? Nothing shocks us! We have become numb!

INDESCENT EXPOSURE

Continual exposure to the things of this world, rubs the edge off our discernment, and nothing displays the forbidden things of this world like pornography.

~

This is an assignment to destroy you and all that you hold dear in this life and beyond.

By acting on fleshly desires and going against God's Word continually, we callous over our spiritual ears, stopping them up with the things of this fallen world.

> *Hebrews 5:14b*
> *...even those who by reason of use have their senses exercised to discern both good and evil.*

<u>We should make a habit of obeying God in all things,</u> and practice being sensitive to His every leading. Make every effort to hear God's Voice and follow it,[58] rather than fulfilling the wants of your flesh.

This will make you and I stronger Christians and less likely to fall into the traps Satan has set for us along life's way.

> *Galatians 5:16*
> *This I say then, Walk in the Spirit, and ye shall not fulfil the lust of the flesh.*

DON'T GET BURNED

Paul spoke of some in our day that would have their conscience seared or charred over with a hot iron.

> *1 Timothy 4:1-2*
> *1. Now the Spirit speaketh expressly, that in the latter times some shall depart from the faith, giving heed to seducing spirits, and doctrines of devils;*
> *2. Speaking lies in hypocrisy; having their conscience seared with a hot iron;*

Concerning sexual sin (specifically fornication and adultery)

---

58   ...for they know his voice. John 10:4 King James Version / Public domain

Solomon wrote these words.

Proverbs 6:24-28
24. To keep thee from the evil woman, from the flattery of the tongue of a strange woman.
25. Lust not after her beauty in thine heart; neither let her take thee with her eyelids.
26. For by means of a whorish woman a man is brought to a piece of bread: and the adulteress will hunt for the precious life.
27. Can a man take fire in his bosom, and his clothes not be burned?
28. Can one go upon hot coals, and his feet not be burned?

∼

This is not a new strategy, many a good soldier or leader has been lured into the enemy's camp by a seductive beautiful woman.

We cannot allow ourselves to be continually exposed to and influenced by images of nudity, sin and all types of vice without expecting dire consequences.

Ephesians 4:19 ESV
They have become callous and have given themselves up to sensuality, greedy to practice every kind of impurity.

A SOBERING WARNING

Romans 1:24-28
24. Wherefore God also gave them up to uncleanness through

the lusts of their own hearts, to dishonour their own bodies between themselves:

25. Who changed the truth of God into a lie, and worshipped and served the creature more than the Creator, who is blessed for ever. Amen.

26. For this cause God gave them up unto vile affections: for even their women did change the natural use into that which is against nature:

27. And likewise also the men, leaving the natural use of the woman, burned in their lust one toward another; men with men working that which is unseemly, and receiving in themselves that recompence of their error which was meet.

28. And even as they did not like to retain God in their knowledge, God gave them over to a reprobate mind, to do those things which are not convenient;

Then after listing several sins, Paul ends with this statement.

Romans 1:32
Who knowing the judgment of God, that they which commit such things are worthy of death, not only do the same, but have pleasure in them that do them.

Here's my translation of the above verse:

Romans 1:32 (modern paraphrase)
They know God disapproves, and that they who are doing such evil things are going to Hell, yet they not only do the same sins, but enjoy viewing them commit their sinful acts on TV, video and in magazines.

For it is a shame even to speak of
those things which are done of them in secret.
Ephesians 5:12

Chapter 6

Modern Problems

Compromise has become the name badge of many churches today. **Our moral guard has been dropped for years:** the devil has used this as an inroad to bring in all sorts of modern spiritual weaponry.

A SHORT HISTORY

In 1938 Honesdale, Pennsylvania banned wearing shorts. One government leader told a local newspaper,[59] "Honesdale is a modest town, not a bathing beach."

Then in 1944 the city of Monahans, Texas followed by passing an ordinance banning women from wearing shorts in public.[60]

There was other communities and cities acrosss America that took a strong stance against the perceived over-exposure of the human body. Even as late as 1959 the city of Plattsburgh, New York[61] voted to ban shorts being worn by anyone over 16 years old in public.

---

59   the Moberly Monitor-Index in Missouri reporting
60   According to The New York Times
61   May 1959 the Associated Press (AP) noted

While some modern day critics may see such ordinances as narrow or over zealous, at least the lawmakers of that day attempted to hold back the floodgates of flesh many suspected was coming. History would prove out; in spite of their best efforts, the gates would soon burst wide open anyway.

THE BIKINI

This small 2-piece women's bathing suit was named after the Bikini[62] Atoll (a small string of islands in the Marshall Islands where the United States tested over 20 nuclear detonations from 1946 to 1958) **because of its explosive effect on the men viewing them.**

<u>Named 'Bikini' because of their explosive effect on the men viewing them.</u> Think about that: bombs are MADE TO KILL!

~

Our moral guard has been dropped for years: the devil has used this as an inroad to bring in all sorts of modern spiritual weaponry.

Most men, especially younger men[63] already battle urges, sexual energy, and fleshly lusts continually. Without having a near nude female body paraded before them.

> Proverbs 6:25
> *Lust not after her beauty in thine heart; neither let her take thee with her eyelids.*

---

62 "Bikini" Encyclopædia Britannica by The Editors of Encyclopædia Britannica / Published May 15, 2015 / https://www.britannica.com/place/Bikini-atoll-Marshall-Islands
63 Flee also youthful lusts. 2 Timothy 2:22 King James Version / Public domain

There is a great book out on the subject of men battling lustful thoughts and images. It is called 'EVERY MAN'S BATTLE - Winning the War on Sexual Temptation One Victory at a Time' *by Stephen Arterburn and Fred Stoeker.*[64]

The book makes this statement,

"American men are in a tough position. They live in a culture awash with sensual images available twenty-four hours a day through a variety of media. It is virtually impossible to avoid such temptations…but, thankfully, not impossible to rise above them."

Job said,

Job 31:1
I made a covenant with mine eyes; why then should I think upon a maid?

THE LAST ACT OF DECENCY

Most have heard of the 'Bondi Bikini Wars' that took place at Bondi Beach[65] in New South Wales, Australia from before 1940 up until the early 60's.

In 1935 The Local Government Act, Ordinance No 52 set exact dimensions for swimming costumes which remained in force until 1961. This meant "men's and women's costumes must have legs at least 3" long, must completely cover the front of the body from a line at the level of the armpits to the waist, have shoul-

---

64   'EVERY MAN'S BATTLE - Winning the War on Sexual Temptation One Victory at a Time' *by Stephen Arterburn and Fred Stoeker* / The Crown Publishing Group / 01/20/2004
65   Bondi 'Bikini Wars' – Arrests on Sydney Beaches (1940s – 1960s) / http://www.xplore-sydney.com

der straps or other means of keeping the costume in position." If these conditions weren't met, the offending person was ordered from the beach, forced to undress and change into 'decent clothes', and was then arrested.

In 1951, American Actress Jean Parker was forcibly escorted from the beach and arrested because her bikini was too skimpy.

66 YEARS LATER

My how times have changed, compromised and deteriorated!

In 2017 women dressed in bikini tops can be seen walking down the street, relaxing in the park or even shopping at the local mall. Not to mention the more than 30 countries that have nude or clothing optional beaches.

The world has seemingly turned a blind eye, along with their blinded hearts to the truth; men and women's bodies are to be saved for their husband or wife. Although clothing around the world often follows the dictates of the climate, **our bodies were not created to be on display for any and all to view.**

> *Titus 2:3-5*
> *3. The aged women likewise, that they be in behaviour as becometh holiness, not false accusers, not given to much wine, teachers of good things;*
> *4. That they may teach the young women to be sober, to love their husbands, to love their children,*
> *5. To be discreet, chaste, keepers at home, good, obedient to their own husbands, that the word of God be not blasphemed.*

To some, seeing way too much exposed skin is normal, but as evidenced by the verses above and the following section of Scriptures <u>God is NOT in agreement with the world's opinion.</u>

THE WORD ON DRESS

The Bible says, "No! It is not right. Put some clothes on!"

In the beginning when Adam and Eve sinned they realized they were naked, so God gave them clothing.

Genesis 3:21
*Unto Adam also and to his wife did the LORD God make coats of skins, **and clothed them.***

The writer of Proverbs once when describing a evil promiscuous woman said...

Proverbs 7:10
And, behold, there met him a woman with the attire of an harlot, and subtil of heart.

The New Living Translation of the Bible defines *'the attire of an harlot'* as *'seductively dressed'*: <u>the NIV calling it **'dressed like a prostitute.'**</u>

When Jesus cast the devils out of the naked madman of Gadara, The Gospel account records, or should I say The Spirit of God chose to make mention of an interesting truth.

Mark 15:5
And they come to Jesus, and see him that was possessed with

*the devil, and had the legion, sitting, **and clothed**, and in his right mind: and they were afraid.*

The Apostle Paul wrote to the Church at Corinth,

> *1 Corinthians 6:19-20*
> *19. What? know ye not that your body is the temple of the Holy Ghost which is in you, which ye have of God, and ye are not your own?*
> *20. For ye are bought with a price: therefore glorify God in your body, and in your spirit, which are God's.*

S.I. MAKES IT SPECIAL

The persuasive power of the media is a modern phenomenon, their ability to tell or present a story (whether good or bad) in a way designed to influence or manipulate the public and then sell it to that same public is nothing short of supernatural.

The dark forces of the enemy have effectively used this power to deceive many. Creative writing, glamorous photos and adventurous tales paint pictures of sin being attractive and fun.

But it's ALL a deception - A LIE!

Magazines like *Sports Illustrated*,[66] *Cosmopolitan*[67] and *Esquire*[68] all pump out their own brand of softcore porn, the later two becoming increasingly more risqué in their articles, photo jou-

---

66   Sports Illustrated / Brendan Ripp / New York, USA / http://www.SI.com
67   Cosmopolitan / Hearst / http://www.cosmopolitan.com
68   Esquire / Hearst Companies / New York, New York USA / http://www.esquire.com

nalism, and celebrated (by the world) Special Editions. These publishing giants sell a watered-down exploitation of flesh, that a compromised public gobbles up at the newstand.

MANY THINK THEY ARE OKAY?

Most Christian men will deny ever having looked at hardcore pornography, and I pray for their sakes that is true. Yet still many of these same men know far more about Hollywood's sex symbols like *Angelina, Pamela* and *Jessica* than they do about Peter, James and John of The Bible? How sad!

~

Proverbs 6:25
Lust not after her beauty in thine heart; neither let her take thee with her eyelids.

1 John 2:15
Love not the world, neither the things that are in the world. If any man love the world, the love of the Father is not in him.

For the millions of men and boys who read the sexy articles and oogle the scantly clad models, this fascination with flesh is just a skip and a jump from the evils of viewing full blown adult pornography.

These men should be reminded of King David's words recorded in The Bible...

Psalms 101:3
I will set no wicked thing before mine eyes: I hate the work of them that turn aside; it shall not cleave to me.

BAIT & SNAGGED

Restaurant chains like *Hooters,*[69] *Twin Peaks,*[70] *the Tilted Kilt,*[71] *Brickhouse Tavern*[72] *and others* (also known as "breastaurants") serve up their own brand of spice. Catering to a mostly male customer base and all aspects of the male appetite; a tantalizing mix of food, worldly fun and flesh.

All of these are mere hooks to get hold of men's flesh, so they can be reeled and dragged into deeper and deeper sexual waters and the slaughter of the devil's lustful nets.

GOD KNOWS THE TRUTH

When we finally stand before a living HOLY God, we will find out that newsstand 'Special Edition' we just had to purchase wasn't so special after all. **God is not fooled, He knows,** fantastic 'hot wings' weren't the only reason you ate lunch there!

2 Peter 2:14a
Having eyes full of adultery, and that cannot cease from sin...

Psalms 96:13
Before the LORD: for he cometh, for he cometh to judge the earth: he shall judge the world with righteousness, and the people with his truth.

---

69   Hooters / Atlanta, GA. / http://www.hooters.com

70   Twin Peaks [Restaurant franchise] Addison, Tx. / http://www.twinpeaksrestaurant.com / Wikipedia, The Free Encyclopedia, 17 Jan. 2017 Accessed 03/08/17

71   Tilted Kilt / founded in Las Vegas, Nevada / Headquarters: Tempe, AZ. / http://www.tiltedkilt.com / http://illuminatimindcontrol.com/breastaurant-hottest-trend-casual-dining/

72   Brickhouse Tavern / Ignite Restaurant Group / Houston TX 77042 / brickhousetavernandtap.com

The Bible makes it very clear that God knows us better[73] than we know ourselves. He knows our hearts and He knows every thought and desire whether good or bad. Our actions declare to the world around us what is in our heart; intentions God knew about the entire time.

We know God is the only all-knowing righteous judge; but both the world and God will judge us for sin (actions in disobedience to His Will.) The world's judgement will be in condemnation: God's judgement will be in righteousness. **<u>Therefore, don't sin!</u>** Do your utmost to never act on lustful thoughts.

> *Romans 6:12*
> *Let not sin therefore reign in your mortal body, that ye should obey it in the lusts thereof.*

> *Hebrews 10:30b-31*
> *30. ... And again, The Lord shall judge his people.*
> *31. It is a fearful thing to fall into the hands of the living God.*

Martin Luther[74] once said, *"You cannot keep birds from flying over your head, but you can keep them from building a nest in your hair"*

CAST THEM DOWN

In other words don't dwell on those thoughts, instead of allowing your mind to wander in the ways of the world, **make your thoughts line up with the Word of God.**

---

73 ... a discerner of the thoughts and intents of the heart. Hebrews 4:12 King James Version
74 goodreads.com "Martin Luther"

2 Corinthians 10:3-5
3. For though we walk in the flesh, we do not war after the flesh:
4. (For the weapons of our warfare are not carnal, but mighty through God to the pulling down of strong holds;)
5. Casting down imaginations, and every high thing that exalteth itself against the knowledge of God, and bringing into captivity every thought to the obedience of Christ;

This will safeguard us against temptation; pure thoughts make for a holy life. **If we judge our thought life, then God will not have to judge our actions.**

DON'T JUDGE ME!

Another compelling truth in The Word of God i.e., many times in The Bible when people came under judgement, God would declare He would expose their nakedness, e.g.

Isaiah 47:3
Thy nakedness shall be uncovered, yea, thy shame shall be seen: I will take vengeance, and I will not meet thee as a man.

Nahum 3:5
Behold, I am against thee, saith the LORD of hosts; and I will discover thy skirts upon thy face, and I will shew the nations thy nakedness, and the kingdoms thy shame. (cf. Ezek 16:36-37, 23:18, 29)

If we take this truth literally; Should we mark those within the porn industry and those standing close enough to peer in already under God's judgement? Whether this assumption is accurate or not—it is still a most sobering thought.

Now concerning the things whereof ye wrote unto me:
It is good for a man not to touch a woman.
I Corinthians 7:1

Chapter 7

Men & Women

We know from the Genesis account, God created man and woman; that same God also created *sex*. Men and women are sexual beings, it is part of our makeup; our character. As humans we are either one sex (male) or the other (female), different, yet the same. For most people being sexual means; sex is on our mind ...and it is on our minds often.

NATURAL DESIRE

Genesis 1:27-28a
27. So God created man in his own image, in the image of God created he him; male and female created he them.
28. And God blessed them, and God said unto them, Be fruitful, and multiply, and replenish the earth...

The command was given by God Himself to procreate, and humans don't do that by osmosis. I believe that when God gave this command to be fruitful and multiply, the natural desire *(sex drive)* was ignited in humans to draw them to each other. Without this natural sexual attraction to the opposite sex men and women wouldn't have carried out God's command to replenish the earth. With currently some 6 billion people on this planet, it is evident this natural attraction and desire has worked quite well.

WITHIN THE MARRIAGE

We will look at 'Marriage' in a later chapter, but for now let's understand that **God intended the sexual union to happen between <u>one man and one woman within the confines of the marriage covenant;</u> God has blessed sex between a man and his wife.**[75] **Any type of sexual activity outside**[76] **of that covenant was and is still, condemned by God's Word as sin.** This is not a popular teaching (no one likes to be told they are wrong) but it is THE TRUTH.

> *Deuteronomy 28:4a*
> *Blessed shall be the fruit of thy body...*

> *Genesis 2:25*
> *And they were both naked, the man and his wife, and were not ashamed.*

It is obvious God has no problem with the sex act as long as it stays within the marriage. Any thorough study of Proverbs, Ecclesiastes, I Corinthians, Ephesians or certainly Song of Solomon will confirm; that **<u>God ordained sex for husbands and wives.</u>**

---

75   Live joyfully with the wife whom thou lovest ... Ecclesiastes 9:9 / Marriage is honourable in all, and the bed undefiled ... Hebrews 13:4 King James Version / Public Domain
76   ... the body is not for fornication / Flee fornication... 1 Corinthians 6:14, 18

Proverbs 5:18-19
18. Let thy fountain be blessed: and rejoice with the wife of thy youth.
19. Let her be as the loving hind and pleasant roe; let her breasts satisfy thee at all times; and be thou ravished always with her love.

BURNING DOWN THE HOUSE

But just like most things God gives to mankind, we have messed this one up also. Men have took this natural sexual desire to the extreme, and in so doing, humans have drove a beautiful hand-crafted very costly luxury vehicle, off into a cheap, filthy, perverted, ditch.

Sexual intercourse is exclusively reserved for one man and one woman within the boundaries of the marriage covenant.

~

God has blessed sex between a man and his wife. Any type of sexual activity outside of that covenant was and is still, condemned by God's Word as sin.

Consider this, a fire is an illuminating, warmth giving, beautiful thing inside the fireplace. But that same fire (even a spark) out on the carpet will BURN YOUR HOUSE DOWN! destroying it and everything in it.

Proverbs 6:25-28
25. Lust not after her beauty in thine heart; neither let her

take thee with her eyelids.
26. For by means of a whorish woman a man is brought to a
piece of bread: and the adulteress will hunt for the precious life.
27. Can a man take fire in his bosom, and his clothes not be
burned?
28. Can one go upon hot coals, and his feet not be burned?

EYE CANDY

Men as a rule, are visually stimulated much more so than women. This makes men especially vunerable to sexual images: photos, videos, etc. The media, advertisers and those within the porn industry know this and they play on this vunerability to drive sales.

They know, Bertha in her curlers and muumuu[77] won't get anyone's attention, but Betty in a bikini will. My Grandpa always said, *"If they have to put a half-dressed pretty woman in the ad to sell their product, it must not be a very good product."*

While I agree with his accessment, in this fallen world's system, a blonde in a pink teddy, or skimpy bathing suit will draw men's attention (and their money) like a moth to a flame. I never realized the following verses were so prophetic until I began writing this book.

Proverbs 6:26a
26. For by means of a whorish woman a man is brought to a
piece of bread...

---

77   muumuu [mu:mu:] is a loose dress of Hawaiian origin that hangs from the shoulder. / Wikipedia, The Free Encyclopedia. Accessed 3/09/17

Ezekiel 16:33
They give gifts to all whores: but thou givest thy gifts to all thy lovers, and hirest them, that they may come unto thee on every side for thy whoredom.

It works much like a well rehearsed male and female pick-pocket team; while the beautiful young lady shows off some of her body and flirts, her male accomplice quietly takes all of the awe-struck victim's money.

Men, we must guard our eye-gate, our money, our mind, and we must in every circumstance guard our heart!

Matthew 5:28
But I say unto you, That whosoever looketh on a woman to lust after her hath committed adultery with her already in his heart.

TWISTING IMAGES

Psalms 139:14
I will praise thee; for I am fearfully and wonderfully made: marvellous are thy works; and that my soul knoweth right well.

That beautiful woman you saw in town, God created her; that cute little cashier at the store, God created her. He took special care to form and fashion her in such a way that a natural attraction would spark between her and the husband God has picked for her. She was made to be attractive to that man. Her feminine attributes and sex appeal were created for her husband.

She was not created so her nude photos could be plastered all over the pages of some cheap magazine. God did not take the time to create her, just so you or I could stare and drool over her, acting like some kind of filthy animal in rut![78] Men and women participating in any part of such base activities are being manipulated by A LIE!

Pornography attacks men and women who were created in the image of God. <u>It distorts God's creation, twisting (perverting) men's perception of that creation;</u> thereby attacking God Himself. This distortion comes as make-up, airbrushing, photoshopping and specific camera angles are used just to make one model, or one short scene look seductive. These tools of the Hollywood 'artists', are used to paint an image of some make-believe dream model onto the canvas of the viewer's mind. Whether that model is male or female the goal is the same; create a desire/a lust[79] for more, thereby creating another customer—hooked on PORNOGRAPHY'S BIG LIE!

---

78   rut - the periodically recurring sexual excitement of the deer, goat, sheep, etc. / Dictionary. com. Dictionary.com Unabridged. Random House, Inc. http://www.dictionary.com/browse/rut

79   Rev. Creflo Dollar described 'lust' as a desire that could not be lawfully fulfilled.

Woe unto them that call evil good, and good evil;
that put darkness for light, and light for darkness;
that put bitter for sweet, and sweet for bitter!
Isaiah 5:20

Chapter 8

Making Love

The devil has perverted one of the most beautiful words ever spoken or written; that word is *love*. Satan has twisted its different meanings and perverted both its applications and uses. The world has bought into his lies and continues to expand and promote the deception.

Thank God, **He has provided His Word so that we don't have to be deceived.** There is truth, solid ground to stand on and time tested answers to every question in life, if we will just take the time to look. All the seductive tricks of this old world are powerful reasons to **READ THE BIBLE; It is the best defense against confusion, traps and deception.**

John 8:32
And ye shall know the truth, and the truth shall make you free.

2 Timothy 2:15
Study to shew thyself approved unto God, a workman that needeth not to be ashamed, rightly dividing the word of truth.

4 KINDS OF LOVE

A truth people must understand is; there are four distinctly different forms of love described in the Greek language: *agapē, éros, phileō* and *storgē;* only two of these are used in Scripture.[80]

▶ *agapē* refers to the love of God;[81] love that motivates to demonstrative action

1) true love: God is love

2) has little to do with emotion or feelings. *agapē* is more about a decision to love; loving as an act of will - commitment, obedience

3) love of God for man and of man for God.

(*cf. Mat 5:43-44; Jo 3:16, 13:34-35, 14:21, 15:12, 21:15; 1 Co 13:4-8; 2 Co 5:14; Gal 5:22; Jam 2:8*)

▶ *eros* is the physical, sensual love between a husband and wife; sexual love or passionate love

1) mostly of the sexual passion. *[The Modern Greek word "erotas" means "intimate love."]*

NOTE: From *eros* comes our modern word *erotic* or *erotica.* As a proper noun it literally was referring to the Greek god of physical or sexual love; the love act. This is one form of the word love that is NOT in the King James Version of the Bible. However the Bible does allude to use of this word most obviously in *Sg of Sol 1:1-4.*

▶ *phileō*[82] is to affectionately love; loving kindness toward a

---

80   Many of the references used in this segue '4 KINDS OF LOVE' were retrieved from The Blue Letter Bible online / http://www.blueletterbible.org / Accessed 2015

81   *agapē* [the love of God] wikipedia.com

82   *phileō* / http://www.biblestudytools.com

friend; to befriend
> 1) to show signs of love and affection -- to kiss (translated as the '*kiss*' 3 different times in the KJV Bible)
> 2) fondness as a friend
> (*cf. Mat 6:5, 10:37; Jo 5:20, 11:2, 35-36, 12:25, 21:15; 1 Co 16:22*)

▶ *storgē*[83] is the natural love and affection between parents, their children, siblings, and exists between husbands and wives in a good marriage.

This form of love is never used in the KJV Bible, except as part of a compound Greek word *philostorgos* in the Book of Romans[84] where the Apostle Paul is admonishing other believers to operate in brotherly love.
> 1) common or natural empathy
> 2) acceptance

GOD'S LOVE MAP

Agapē (love) motivates a man or woman to the mission field. It allows a Christian to love the unloveable, to continue reaching out, giving, and ministering, when their extended hand is rejected or even bitten. That's the God-kind of love!

Eros (love) is all about the physical expression of one's romantic feelings toward another (lawfully) their spouse or (unlawfully) toward a lover outside the covering of a marriage covenant.

Phileō (love) is what an individual has for a friend, a comrade or buddy. It can be very strong, e.g., between best friends, life-long coworkers, fellow soldiers or law enforcement partners, etc...

---

83 *storgē* / http://www.truthortradition.com
84 Be kindly affectioned one to another with brotherly love... Romans 12:10a

Storgē (love) is family, the deep heartfelt love one has for their spouse and their children.

THINK ABOUT THIS - I can have and demonstrate *Agapē* and *Phileō* for a friend. Likewise I can have and should demonstrate *Agapē* and *Storgē* for my children. But I can have all 4 types of love *Agapē, Storgē, Phileō* and *Eros* for my wife. She is or should be all of the following to me: my sister in Christ, my best friend and my lover; she completes me. Therefore **marriage is the best picture of God's Love Map for humanity.**

> 1 John 4:8
> *He that loveth not knoweth not God; **for God is love.***

BAD INFORMATION

We live in a society which has been wrongly educated, and terribly misinformed about love. The constant barrage of erotic images and misinformation about relationships from various media has successfully brainwashed the public to the point most think love cannot exist without *eros*.

~

All the seductive tricks of this old world are powerful reasons to READ THE BIBLE; It is the best defense against confusion, traps and deception.

People funnel every thought about love and relationships through an *eros* or erotic filter, e.g., "she's hot" or "he's a stud!" "Will she do this or that in bed?" "Was he or she good?" **This is not how**

God intended humans to operate! This is PERVERSION!

SODOM'S SINS

This was the lifestyle in Sodom[85] before it was destroyed and this was the condition of the world before the great flood.[86]

Genesis 6:5
And GOD saw that the wickedness of man was great in the earth, and that every imagination of the thoughts of his heart was only evil continually.

Genesis 19:4-7
4. But before they lay down, the men of the city, even the men of Sodom, compassed the house round, both old and young, all the people from every quarter:
*5. And they called unto Lot, and said unto him, Where are the men which came in to thee this night? bring them out unto us, **that we may know**[87] **them.***
6. And Lot went out at the door unto them, and shut the door after him,
7. And said, I pray you, brethren, do not so wickedly.

But human beings don't seem to learn from their past mistakes. Even Jesus in a prophecy about the last days, likened the sinful condition of our day with that of Noah's. THINK ABOUT IT!

---

85   Genesis 10:19 'Sodom' A city of ancient Palestine possibly located south of the Dead Sea. (n.d.) American Heritage® Dictionary of the English Language, Fifth Edition. (2011). http://www.thefreedictionary.com/Sodom
86   Genesis 6:17 [flood of Noah] approximately 4,359 years ago in the year 1656 AM or 2348 BC / David Wright, AiG–U.S. / http://www.answersingenesis.org
87   *"we may know them"* [to know (a person carnally] Source: Blue Letter Bible online / http://www.blueletterbible.org

Matthew 24:37-39

37. But as the days of Noe were, so shall also the coming of the Son of man be.

38. For as in the days that were before the flood they were eating and drinking, marrying and giving in marriage, until the day that Noe entered into the ark,

39. And knew not until the flood came, and took them all away; so shall also the coming of the Son of man be.

BLINDED MEN

Genesis 19:10-11

10. But the men put forth their hand, and pulled Lot into the house to them, and shut to the door.

11. And they smote the men that were at the door of the house with blindness, both small and great: so that they wearied themselves to find the door.

No doubt the angels knew there was no reasoning with the sin-laden men of Sodom and they[88] pulled Lot into the house for his own safety.

Blinded because of their overwhelming perverted desires they wearied (or wore themselves to a frazzle) trying to find the door. Let that soak in a minute—they couldn't find access into the righteous house because of consequences of their sin.

I heard one minister from Tennessee, who had worked with thousands of mental patients say, *"I've not dealt with one, not one single patient either male or female that had lost their mind, who*

---

88   For he shall give his angels charge over thee... Psalms 91:11; Luke 4:10

had not been doing something or allowing someone to do crazy perverted things to their body."

Then he told of a college student who had streaked across a college campus, then his mind snapped and he was like a vegetable for months before he finally was set free through a deliverance ministry. Then he shared about a girl who had sex with multiple partners and became trapped in her own world of imaginary friends and wild hallucinations.

Please, PLEASE I beg you, don't flirt with sin! The relationship you are courting is with Satan, and it is only consumated in much evil and <u>personal destruction</u>.

Romans 6:15
Know ye not, that to whom ye yield yourselves servants to obey, his servants ye are to whom ye obey; whether of sin unto death, or of obedience unto righteousness?

2 Corinthians 4:4
In whom <u>the god of this world hath blinded the minds of them</u> which believe not, lest the light of the glorious gospel of Christ, who is the image of God, should shine unto them.

IDENTITY CRISIS

The media's mis-education has so influenced people, that many have little to no self-esteem or identity outside of the sexual realm. Women and teenage girls have expensive makeovers and practice extreme dieting all to keep a certain look. A look they have been trained to think is beautiful, hot and sexy. They have to maintain what their perceived vision of the perfect woman is, or they get withdrawn, depressed or even suicidal.

The world has its names: "This girl is easy," "that woman is a cougar" or "that guy is a player." All these terms are wrapped around one subject—SEX!

The Bible uses other terms for such sexual sins.

> *1 Corinthians 6:9*
> *Know ye not that the unrighteous shall not inherit the kingdom of God? Be not deceived: neither fornicators, nor idolaters, nor adulterers, nor effeminate, nor abusers of themselves with mankind,*

~

If that man truly loves you, he will wait for you. Keep yourself pure!

For many others, their identity issues are a curse they battle daily. One person doesn't know if he is a woman or a man, still another cannot think of love without the vilest and most perverted of sexual acts invading his or her mind.

All of this is confusion and deception brought in by the enemy to rewrite God's Love Map. **He wants to kill, steal and destroy**[89] **men and women's lives, ruin their families and extinguish their divine destiny.**

---

89   ...but for to steal, and to kill, and to destroy... John 10:10 King James Version

TWISTED SISTERS

2 Timothy 3:6
For of this sort are they which creep into houses, and lead cap-
tive silly women laden with sins, led away with divers lusts,

This continual pressure on women to be pretty, shapely, and sexy is designed to push women to the limit. Satan wants to push girls and women off the edge of reality, and he doesn't really care which edge they fall from. He is just happy if they fall or become: depressed, a mental patient, a victim of disease, raped, addicted to sex, addicted to drugs or alcohol, become a lesbian, are left alone, lost or even dead.

Listen to me women, the devil is PLAYING FOR KEEPS! so avoid all exposure or involvement with pornography and illicit sex. Make the decision to **KEEP YOURSELF PURE!**

NO RING, NO FLING!

Insecure and looking desperately for approval, many a young woman has sold herself out for a moment of pleasure with who she thought was the man of her dreams, only to later realize he was the stuff of nightmares. TRUTH - **If that man truly loves you, he will wait for you. KEEP YOURSELF PURE!** I cannot stress this enough!

Trade your future for only a few minutes of pleasure? It's just not worth the risk of: an unwanted pregnancy, your morality marred for life, a deadly disease or even putting your eternal destiny in jeopardy? Think about it! **KEEP YOURSELF PURE!**

The Apostle Paul addressing marriage and sex wrote this.

> *1 Corinthians 7:1-2 NLT*
> *1. Now regarding the questions you asked in your letter. Yes, it is good to abstain from sexual relations.*
> *2. But because there is so much sexual immorality, each man should have his own wife, and each woman should have her own husband.*

> *1 Corinthians 7:9 NLT*
> *But if they can't control themselves, they should go ahead and marry. It's better to marry than to burn with lust.*

MORE THAN THAT

Our identity or should I say, our true identity only comes from a relationship with God through Jesus Christ and a understanding of Who He is and who we are in Him. There is no other source of identity, confidence, love, peace or joy; **Jesus is the answer.**

God Himself designed mankind in His image, we were designed to walk in perfect fellowship with our heavenly Father. But when Adam and Eve sinned, their identity or the way they identified themselves in relation to The Father was marred, so much so, that when God walked in the garden, they felt so condemned by their own disobedience (sin) they hid from Him in fear.

> *Genesis 3:8-10*
> *8. And they heard the voice of the LORD God walking in the garden in the cool of the day: and Adam and his wife hid themselves from the presence of the LORD God amongst the trees of the garden.*

9. *And the LORD God called unto Adam, and said unto him, Where art thou?*
10. *And he said, I heard thy voice in the garden, and I was afraid, because I was naked; and I hid myself.*

THE AGAPĒ OF GOD

John 3:16
For God so loved the world, that he gave his only begotten Son, that whosoever believeth in him should not perish, but have everlasting life.

Matthew 24:12
And because iniquity shall abound, the love of many shall wax cold.

The world and even many in The Church, do not understand the love of God. Some think they do, but when pressed, it quickly becomes clear they have mistaken *storgē* (natural love) as *agapē* love that only comes from God.

~

There is no other source of identity, confidence, love, peace or joy; Jesus is the answer.

Agapē love gives unselfishly, even to those who are unreceptive with no want of recognition, repayment or reward. *Agapē* is pure, unselfish in its actions and motive. *Agapē* has no hidden agenda, it is transparent with its only goal to help and love unconditionally.

PAUL WROTE ABOUT LOVE

1 Corinthians 13:1-8, 13 NLT
1. If I could speak all the languages of earth and of angels, but didn't love others, I would only be a noisy gong or a clanging cymbal.
2. If I had the gift of prophecy, and if I understood all of God's secret plans and possessed all knowledge, and if I had such faith that I could move mountains, but didn't love others, I would be nothing.
3. If I gave everything I have to the poor and even sacrificed my body, I could boast about it; but if I didn't love others, I would have gained nothing.
4. Love is patient and kind. Love is not jealous or boastful or proud
5. or rude. It does not demand its own way. It is not irritable, and it keeps no record of being wronged.
6. It does not rejoice about injustice but rejoices whenever the truth wins out.
7. Love never gives up, never loses faith, is always hopeful, and endures through every circumstance.
8. Prophecy and speaking in unknown languages and special knowledge will become useless. But love will last forever!

13. Three things will last forever—faith, hope, and love—and the greatest of these is love.

Marriage is honourable in all,
and the bed undefiled:
but whoremongers and adulterers God will judge.
Hebrews 13:4

Chapter 9

The Marriage Bed

God is not haphazard or confused about relationships, love, intimacy or sex. He has a plan that brings order to this world's mindless chaos, when we choose to do things— His way.

COVENANT[90]

God is a covenant God; He made a covenant with Abraham; He made a covenant with Jesus, and He designed a covenant for marriage. A covenant or contract (a promise) of blessing, protection and provision bestowed on two people (a husband and a wife) whom God Himself joined together in marriage.

One provision of this marriage covenant is the intimacy of the sexual union, thus making two people one flesh (or one person) inside the marriage; one in Christ; one in agreement, walking together strong in the Lord. Look at the following verses.

---

90 'Covenant' a divine promise establishing or modifying God's relationship to humanity / (n.d.) American Heritage® Dictionary of the English Language, Fifth Edition. (2011). Retrieved March 10 2017 from http://www.thefreedictionary.com

Ephesians 5:29-31
28. So ought men to love their wives as their own bodies. He that loveth his wife loveth himself.
29. For no man ever yet hated his own flesh; but nourisheth and cherisheth it, even as the Lord the church:
30. For we are members of his body, of his flesh, and of his bones.
31. For this cause shall a man leave his father and mother, and shall be joined unto his wife, and they two shall be one flesh.

Ecclesiastes 4:12
And if one prevail against him, two shall withstand him; and a threefold cord is not quickly broken.

Pornography makes a mockery of the marriage covenant, portraying the sexual union as the ultimate gratification between a man and a woman. True love, intimacy, heartfelt romance, bonding, growing together, building a family, are all thrown out and God's beautiful plan for a couple is totally disregarded.

LIKE A VIRGIN

Deuteronomy 22:15
Then shall the father of the damsel, and her mother, take and bring forth the tokens[91] of the damsel's virginity unto the elders of the city in the gate:

Normally the hymen[92] of a virgin is ruptured or torn, causing

---

91 'tokens' a blood-stained sheet or cloth from the bed where a marriage is consummated. The blood (dam betulim) is said to "prove" the bride's virginity... / Peter C. Craigie, The Book of Deuteronomy (NICOT; Grand Rapids: Eerdmans, 1976), 292-293 [online] http://hermeneutics.stackexchange.com/questions

92 a fold of mucous membrane partly closing the external orifice of the vagina in a virgin. / hymen. (n.d.). Dictionary.com Unabridged. Retrieved March 13, 2017

some bleeding the first time she has sexual intercourse. Since many weddings of that day were arranged: This blood on the sheets was used as evidence (a token) of her virginity should her new husband or anyone else question the bride's chastity, her integrity, or her family's integrity.

There are a multitude of analogies and lessons we can learn from this, e.g., the blood speaks, the life is in the blood, a living sacrifice, the veil being torn, etc. But for the purpose of this writing, I want to expand on what that blood says.

The blood spilled on the sheets, tells her husband you are the only one; it says you are the only man that has ever touched me in this way. It says you have entered into my flesh and we are one.

~

This is all part of the melding together of two hearts, two minds, two people into one whole.

The revelation here is: You (Christ) have broken-down the wall of my flesh, You have free entrance into every area of my life, and (the life's in the blood) that life is given (submitted) to You.

The Apostle Paul wrote the following:

2 Corinthians 11:2 RSV
I feel a divine jealousy for you, for I betrothed[93] you to Christ to present you as a pure bride to her one husband.

---

93 'betrothed' to join or marry; the King James Version uses the word 'espoused' / Source: Blue Letter Bible online / http://www.blueletterbible.org

Romans 12:1
I beseech you therefore, brethren, by the mercies of God,
that ye present your bodies a living sacrifice, holy, accept-
able unto God, which is your reasonable service.

AFFAIRS OF THE HEART

Declaring love and devotion to your spouse while still seeing another, would never work. So too, declaring love and devotion for
Christ and then continuing to flirt with the enemy never works
and quickly ends in spiritual disaster. **You cannot expect any
great level of intimacy with your husband, wife, or in your
walk with Christ while you are still sleeping with a devil.**

The spirits behind pornography will never allow a viewer to be
open and free with another. The enemy of men's souls is a hard
taskmaster, selfish and controlling.

Romans 6:15
Know ye not, that to whom ye yield yourselves servants to
obey, his servants ye are to whom ye obey; whether of sin
unto death, or of obedience unto righteousness?

Always remember: **love gives to others, lust takes from others.**
Love wants the truth, but because lust is a lie, it has no problem
continuing in deception and producing more of the same.

When one party is viewing porn regularly, any level of stability,
intimacy, or trust within the relationship is quickly eroded or
destroyed altogether. Why? For one, it's adultery, it may be only
in the mind, but it is still adultery. The imaginary acts, fantasy
liasons and role playing in the mind are very real to the subcon-

scious, and very serious in the spirit. Jesus spoke about the seriousness of sexual fantasies in Matthew.

Matthew 5:27-28
27. Ye have heard that it was said by them of old time, Thou shalt not commit adultery:
28. But I say unto you, That whosoever looketh on a woman to lust after her hath committed adultery with her already in his heart.

Then there is the overwhelming amount of lies and cover-ups the viewer must maintain just to keep their sin secret. Have you ever walked into someone's house and their naughty movies were stacked on the TV and porn magazines all over the coffee table? Of course you haven't, they keep that (those dirty secrets) all hid in the closet or under the mattress. THINK ABOUT IT - If I'm guilty of habitually looking at hardcore porn, I sure don't want my spouse, my children, and certainly not my Christian friends knowing about it. This literally throws intimacy out the door, because I can't afford to let you into my secret place—that's where I hide the dirty books and DVD's.

Numbers 32:23b
... and be sure your sin will find you out.

Luke 12:2
For there is nothing covered, that shall not be revealed; neither hid, that shall not be known.

John 3:20
For every one that doeth evil hateth the light, neither cometh to the light, lest his deeds should be reproved.

INTIMACY

A leading female Evangelist stated about intimacy, "*Intimacy is best explained by breaking apart the word and then saying it, 'into-me-you-see.*" Nothing hidden, naked before one another we are exposed to our spouse completely. This is all part of the melding together of two hearts, two minds, two people into one whole.

Inside the marriage covenant the male-female relationship is truly restored back to its original at the time of creation—one flesh.

Genesis 2:22-25
22. And the rib, which the LORD God had taken from man, made he a woman, and brought her unto the man.
23. And Adam said, This is now bone of my bones, and flesh of my flesh: she shall be called Woman, because she was taken out of Man.
24. Therefore shall a man leave his father and his mother, and shall cleave unto his wife: and they shall be one flesh.
25. And they were both naked, the man and his wife, and were not ashamed.

Jesus said it this way,
Matthew 19:4-6
4. And he answered and said unto them, Have ye not read, that he which made them at the beginning made them male and female,
5. And said, For this cause shall a man leave father and mother, and shall cleave to his wife: and they twain shall be one flesh?
6. Wherefore they are no more twain, but one flesh. What therefore God hath joined together, let not man put asunder.

ABUSING OUR LICENSE

Some overly amorous young groom may boast, *"I'm married, we got a license to act that way. God doesn't care if I swing from the light fixture!"* Well God might not care, but I dare to say, *"Your wife does!"* Did she agree to swing from the fixtures with you? Or does she just want to be emotionally scarred or physically injured when your little porn scene doesn't work out on the stage of your bed the way you imagined it would in the script of your mind?

All too often this type of sexual bravado is the cause of much hurt and division between many husbands and wives. One of the most devastating effects of pornography[94] to a marriage, is that it often sabotages a couple's ability to enjoy a normal sex life. In many cases, the husband or wife isn't interested in sex with his or her partner because they have been so programmed by much higher levels of erotic stimulation they no longer respond to normalcy.[95]

According to Dr. Victor Cline,[96] a clinical psychologist at the University of Utah and a specialist in the area of sexual addictions;
"The pornography consumer, similar to the drug user, requires more and more stimulation to reach his or her "highs." In fact some viewers prefer the powerful sexual im-

---

94 Focus on the Family online / The Impact of Pornography on Marital Sex by Juli Slattery http://www.focusonthcfamily.com/marriage/sex-and-intimacy/when-your-husband-isnt-interested-in-sex/the-impact-of-pornography-on-marital-sex

95 "normalcy" the state of being normal. / Random House Kernerman Webster's College Dictionary, © 2010 K Dictionaries Ltd. Copyright 2005, 1997, 1991 by Random House, Inc. All rights reserved.

96 Cline, Pornography's Effects, 3-5. iiVictor B. Cline, "Pornography and Sexual Addictions," Christian Counseling Today 4, no.4 (1996): 58. https://www.protectkids.com/effects/patternofaddiction.htm

agery planted in their minds by exposure to pornography to sexual intercourse itself. This nearly always diminishes the viewer's capacity to love and express appropriate intimacy within relationships."

We can't use the *'the bed is undefiled'*[97] excuse for sexual activity in the bedroom that in some way, hurts, disrespects or condemns our spouse. **If the sexual act one partner wants to do, places guilt or pain on the other. That's NOT God!**

I like the way The Message Bible translates this verse.

Hebrews 13:4 MSG[98]
Honor marriage, and guard the sacredness of sexual intimacy between wife and husband. God draws a firm line against casual and illicit sex.

NO THREESOMES

In this day and hour you had better guard your marriage and family. Largely due to the amount of sexual imagery being streamed 24/7 into people's lives by a twisted, self-feeding media, there has been an exponential rise in the numbers of sexual predators in our land.

These lust-filled men and women, who are set on fire of hell, want to seduce you, rape your wife, and molest your children. These perverted agents of Satan seek the innocent and the ignorant as victims for their immoral schemes.

---

97 Hebrews 13:4 King James Version / Public domain
98 The Message Bible © 2002 by Eugene H. Peterson / Bible Gateway online / https://www.biblegateway.com

2 Corinthians 2:11
Lest Satan should get an advantage of us: for we are not ig-
norant of his devices.

Don't you dare bring another lover (man or woman) into your
bedroom; not in person, not on paper, not on video, not on your
computer, NOT EVEN IN YOUR MIND! It's an abomination!
It's sin! IT'S A DEVIL!!!

GOD'S PLAN

1 Corinthians 7:2-5 NLT
2. But because there is so much sexual immorality, each man
should have his own wife, and each woman should have her
own husband.
3. The husband should fulfill his wife's sexual needs, and the
wife should fulfill her husband's needs.
4. The wife gives authority over her body to her husband,
and the husband gives authority over his body to his wife.
5. Do not deprive each other of sexual relations, unless you
both agree to refrain from sexual intimacy for a limited time
so you can give yourselves more completely to prayer. After-
ward, you should come together again so that Satan won't
be able to tempt you because of your lack of self-control.

~

If the sexual act one partner wants to do, places guilt or pain on the other. That's NOT God!

Yes, God created sex, yes God put the natural sexual attraction in men and women. But He did this so people could find a suitable mate, fall in love (*storgē*), marry, experience and enjoy *eros* within the confines of the Marriage covenant. By design the married man and woman walk through this life together in the *agapē* of God demonstrating to their children and to everyone around them *phileō* (kindness, good works, compassion and friendship) and *agapē* (the love of God He has for the world He has placed inside every believer.) As I stated in an earlier chapter, **marriage is the best picture of God's Love Map for humanity.** Think on the following verses.

Ecclesiastes 9:9a
Live joyfully with the wife whom thou lovest all the days of the life of thy vanity, which he hath given thee under the sun...

Ephesians 5:25
Husbands, love your wives, even as Christ also loved the church, and gave himself for it;

Wherefore come out from among them, and be ye separate, saith the Lord, and touch not the unclean thing; and I will receive you, And will be a Father unto you, and ye shall be my sons and daughters, saith the Lord Almighty.
2 Corinthians 6:17-18

Chapter 10

Repentance

Perhaps the best definition of repentance[99] is found in *2 Corinthians.*

2 Corinthians 7:11 NKJV
"For observe this very thing, that you sorrowed in a godly manner: What diligence it produced in you, what clearing of yourselves, what indignation, what fear, what vehement desire, what zeal, what vindication! In all things you proved yourselves to be clear in this matter."

OPINIONS VARY

Those who are lost in the porn industry, are blinded and don't understand how a holy God views their sins. To those still in the clutches of the enemy, sin is seen as something fun, adventurous, and even to some degree desireable; after all the Bible tells us sin is fun for a short time.[100] The devil paints a tantalizing picture of all the things this world has to offer.

---

99   Some references retrieved from the La Vista Church of Christ website. Used by Permission. http://lavistachurchofchrist.org/LVanswers/2006/11-02.htm
100   ... enjoy the pleasures of sin for a season; Hebrews 11:25b King James Version

Too many times, especially with sexual sins, people are caught in an illicit act or compromising situation by authorities or sometimes even worse, by a loved one. <u>Then they are sorry for getting caught, but not truly repentant.</u> To truly repent, an individual must see sin as it really is; detestable, wretched, rotten and destructive. Their opinion of sin must change, in other words, they must see it the way God does.

People often have the opinion; I hate I got caught, maybe it will work out better next time, if not, I can always get forgiveness. So they begin to apologize, make amends, beg, deal, etc. anything to work toward an out. But their opinion (their view) hasn't changed! **They are not truly seeking the way,**[101] **they are just looking for a way out.**

> *2 Corinthians 7:10*
> *For godly sorrow worketh repentance to salvation not to be repented of: but the sorrow of the world worketh death.*

God knows the only lasting (eternal) solution is true repentance, a complete denouncing of and turning away from the old life, old friends, old habits, etc. and an accepting of Christ's finished work on the cross. True repentance goes hand in hand with a 180° change of view: 'Repentance' reflects the attitude one brings into conversion, the turning from sin demonstrates the change of thinking (views and opinions) and new direction that comes as a part of it.[102]

The moment this takes place (conversion[103]) the individual not

---

101   Jesus saith unto him, I am the way, the truth, and the life: no man cometh unto the Father, but by me. John 14:6 / Source: Blue Letter Bible online / http://www.blueletterbible.org
102, 103   'conversion' a turning to embrace God / Elwell, Walter A. "Entry for 'Convert, Conversion'". "Evangelical Dictionary of Theology". . 1997.

only sees their dire need of a Savior, but seems to supernaturally understand sin is abominable, filthy, disgusting, and loathesome to The Father and he or she truly hates it at every level.

ANOTHER CHANCE

This new convert in Christ is now changed on the inside, his or her spirit is recreated in Christ Jesus and the days of wallowing in darkness are over. **No matter where they have been or what they have been doing, it is all washed away by the blood of Christ, they are forgiven, a brand new creation in the Kingdom of God.**

> *2 Corinthians 5:17*
> *Therefore if any man be in Christ, he is a new creature: old things are passed away; behold, all things are become new.*

God meant exactly what He said here, "ALL THINGS ARE BECOME NEW." No matter how deep someone has been in the gutter of this old world, no matter how far into drugs, sex, or perversion of any kind; they can have a second chance. **There is nothing the devil can do to a person, that Jesus cannot undo and set that person totally free.**

GETTING RIGHT WITH GOD

▶ God protected Rahab the harlot[104] and her entire family.
▶ God restored King David after his affair[105] with Bathsheba.
▶ God bought back and set free Gomer the adulterous wife[106] of Hosea the Prophet.

---

104   'Rahab the harlot' Joshua 6:17 King James Version / Public domain
105   'King David's affair' 2 Samuel 11:2-27, 12:13, 24 King James Version / Public Domain / Blue Letter Bible online / http://www.blueletterbible.org
106   'Gomer' Hosea 3:1-3 King James Bible / Public domain

► Jesus cast seven devils out of Mary Magdalene[107] and she followed Him the rest of her life.

► Jesus set the naked madman of the Gadarenes[108] free and restored his mind.

► Jesus did not condemn the woman taken in adultery.[109]

God brought those deep in sexual sins out by His incredible mercy and grace, and He will do the same for you.

~

There is nothing the devil can do to a person, that Jesus cannot undo and set that person totally free.

Now your brand new life in Christ Jesus, FREE FROM ALL BONDAGE, is about to begin.

THE ONLY WAY

The Bible says that all men and women are sinners and lost without Christ, they have no chance of fellowshiping with God at any level, not in this life or in the eternal one to come.

Romans 3:23 NLT[110]
For everyone has sinned; we all fall short of God's glorious standard.

---

107 'Mary Magdalene' the woman from whom He had cast out seven demons. Mk 16:9 NLT

108 'madman of the Gadarenes' Luke 8:26-36 King James Version / Public domain

109 'woman taken in adultery' John 8:3-11 King James version / Public Domain

110 All of "The Roman Road to Salvation" verses taken from the New Living Translation of the Bible / For everyone has sinned we." Blue Letter Bible. Web. 16 Mar, 2017. <https://www.blueletterbible.org/nlt/rom/3/23/s_1049023>.

Romans 6:23 NLT
For the wages of sin is death, but the free gift of God is eternal life through Christ Jesus our Lord.

But the GOOD NEWS is: God sent His only Son Jesus to become a sacrifice to pay for your sins; purchasing with His own blood, your freedom from the grip Satan had on your life through sin.

John 3:16-17 NLT
16. For God loved the world so much that he gave his one and only Son, so that everyone who believes in him will not perish but have eternal life.
17. God sent his Son into the world not to judge the world, but to save the world through him.

The Apostle Paul confirms this powerful life-changing truth in his writings[111] both to the Romans and the church at Corinth.

Romans 5:8 NLT
But God showed his great love for us by sending Christ to die for us while we were still sinners.

2 Corinthians 5:21
For God made Christ, who never sinned, to be the offering for our sin, so that we could be made right with God through Christ.

But it didn't end with His death. **Three days later He arose from death, hell, and the grave, VICTORIOUS OVER ALL THE POWER OF THE ENEMY!** This guaranteed our victory

---

111   Dating Paul's letter to the Romans (A.D. 56-58); then writing his 2nd letter to the Corinthian Church between (A.D. 55-57)

forever!</u> Now Jesus is THE ONLY ONE TRUE LIVING SAV-
IOR and can boldly declare these truthes.

John 14:6
Jesus told him, "I am the way, the truth, and the life. No one
can come to the Father except through me.

Romans 10:9-10
9. If you confess with your mouth that Jesus is Lord and be-
lieve in your heart that God raised him from the dead, you
will be saved.
10. For it is by believing in your heart that you are made
right with God, and it is by confessing with your mouth that
you are saved.

Romans 10:13
For "Everyone who calls on the name of the LORD will be saved."

JESUS PLEASE HELP ME!

Do you believe in your heart the verses you've just read? Then
the next step is to pray and confess Jesus as your Lord. Pray this
prayer out loud.

"Dear God,
I recognize that I am a sinner, and I ask for You to forgive
me. I believe Jesus Christ is Your only living Son. I believe
He came to Earth, lived a perfect sinless life as a man. I be-
lieve He was crucified for my sins, and that three days later
You raised Him from the dead, claiming victory over all the
power of the enemy. I trust Him as my Savior and will fol-
low Him as Lord of my life forever.

Jesus, I publicly declare you are LORD OF MY LIFE, please guide my life daily to do your will. Thank You Heavenly Father for loving me so much, and for saving me and delivering me from Satan's traps and bondage. I have asked all this in the Name of Jesus, and I know by faith You have done it.

I am now a Christian FREE in Christ Jesus. Amen. THANK YOU LORD!!!"

NO LONGER A SLAVE TO SIN

The following passages will help you understand what just took place in your life and the new freedom you now have in the Kingdom of God through Christ Jesus.

Romans 5:6-11 NLT
6. When we were utterly helpless, Christ came at just the right time and died for us sinners.
7. Now, most people would not be willing to die for an upright person, though someone might perhaps be willing to die for a person who is especially good.
8. But God showed his great love for us by sending Christ to die for us while we were still sinners.
9. And since we have been made right in God's sight by the blood of Christ, he will certainly save us from God's condemnation.
10. For since our friendship with God was restored by the death of his Son while we were still his enemies, we will certainly be saved through the life of his Son.
11. So now we can rejoice in our wonderful new relationship with God because our Lord Jesus Christ has made us friends of God.

Romans 6:11-23 NLT
11. So you also should consider yourselves to be dead to the power of sin and alive to God through Christ Jesus.
12. Do not let sin control the way you live; do not give in to sinful desires.
13. Do not let any part of your body become an instrument of evil to serve sin. Instead, give yourselves completely to God, for you were dead, but now you have new life. So use your whole body as an instrument to do what is right for the glory of God.
14. Sin is no longer your master, for you no longer live under the requirements of the law. Instead, you live under the freedom of God's grace.
15. Well then, since God's grace has set us free from the law, does that mean we can go on sinning? Of course not!
16. Don't you realize that you become the slave of whatever you choose to obey? You can be a slave to sin, which leads to death, or you can choose to obey God, which leads to righteous living.
17. Thank God! Once you were slaves of sin, but now you wholeheartedly obey this teaching we have given you.
18. Now you are free from your slavery to sin, and you have become slaves to righteous living.
19. Because of the weakness of your human nature, I am using the illustration of slavery to help you understand all this. Previously, you let yourselves be slaves to impurity and lawlessness, which led ever deeper into sin. Now you must give yourselves to be slaves to righteous living so that you will become holy.
20. When you were slaves to sin, you were free from the obligation to do right.
21. And what was the result? You are now ashamed of the

things you used to do, things that end in eternal doom.
22. But now you are free from the power of sin and have
become slaves of God. Now you do those things that lead to
holiness and result in eternal life.
23. For the wages of sin is death, but the free gift of God is
eternal life through Christ Jesus our Lord.

YOUR NEW LIFE

Now find a good Bible teaching, Bible-believing church, and
plug-in to it. Don't just attend, get involved, commit to being
there every service, every time they need members to help, or
have an event or function, make every effort to attend and help.

⌒

"Everyone who calls on the name of the LORD will be saved."

Surround yourself with other believers. **Christianity is a family
and we need each other's support, love and prayers.**

Pray often and study the Bible in private as well as in church,
Sunday School, and mid-week Bible Study, etc. When I first got
saved, I tried to keep a running conversation going with God
throughout the day, and I read my Bible every chance I got: usually morning, evening and during my lunch break.

**A personal daily walk with God is vital to you maintaining
your freedom,** and protecting yourself from Satan's tricks,
traps and snares.

100% CHRISTIAN

This new life in Christ is not something an individual can do part-time with any amount of success. Actually, living a part-time Christianity, will make a person completely miserable.

It has always amazed me how many people serve the devil 'whole hog'; drinking, lies, sex, fights, drugs, etc. I mean the entire gambit, participating in anything Hell has to offer. Then they get saved and immediately start putting on the brakes when it comes to God and church activities?

This is not the way it should be! **As Christians we should be the most active, alive, and exciting group of people on the planet!** We ought to at least serve the Savior every bit as energetic and dedicated as we served the destroyer! Because, on this team (God's Kingdom) WE WIN!!!

Romans 12:1-2
1. I beseech you therefore, brethren, by the mercies of God, that ye present your bodies a living sacrifice, holy, acceptable unto God, which is your reasonable service.
2. And be not conformed to this world: but be ye transformed by the renewing of your mind, that ye may prove what is that good, and acceptable, and perfect, will of God.

*And have no fellowship with the unfruitful works of darkness,
but rather reprove them.
Ephesians 5:11*

Chapter 11

The Godly Man

[This chapter is dedicated to all the Christian men out there, attending church, praying, studying The Word and making every effort to live their life, maintain their family and work their carreer in purity and holiness.]

CAN'T LIVE IN A BUBBLE

We all know, thanks to Adam and Eve's sin, we now live in a fallen world. It is base, carnal, and tilted toward the darkness in many ways. We have to live, raise our families and work <u>in</u> this world - BUT WE DON'T HAVE TO BE <u>OF</u> THIS WORLD!

John 17:14-16 NIV
14. I have given them your word and the world has hated them, for they are not of the world any more than I am of the world.
15. My prayer is not that you take them out of the world but that you protect them from the evil one.
16. They are not of the world, even as I am not of it.

As Christian men we must guard our heart,[112] be aware of Satan's tricks,[113] and put sin out of our life. But we also must make a distinction between having our guard up, versus being overly guarded: because timid, bubble-wrapped Christians, are not what the world needs right now. If that is the only way one can maintain holiness in their Christian walk, then that person is not praying, reading their Bible enough or fellowshiping with other believers enough to stay strong.

~

Just remember all of Heaven is on your side, and YOU ARE ON THE WINNING TEAM!

What the world needs is strong, Bible believing, Spirit-filled men of God, who will carry their cross into the darkness on one side and bring those headed for hell out on the other side saved, free and now destined for Heaven. This type of bold Christianity requires a very dedicated life, one of much time spent with God, in prayer and in His Word, with a genuine agapē[114] love for hurting people. Not every Christian is called to this type of frontline ministry but for those who are, and who can handle it, their life can be very rewarding.

BLINDERS

What kind of blinders? We can't be blinded to everything in the world, that's being overly guarded as I mentioned earlier.

---

112   Keep thy heart with all diligence; for out of it are the issues of life. Pro 4:23 King James Version / Public Domain

113   Lest Satan should get an advantage of us: for we are not ignorant of his devices. 2 Co 2:11 King James Version / Public Domain

114   agapē - refers to the love of God love that motivates to demonstrative action SEE: Ch. 8 'Making Love' segue '4 KINDS OF LOVE' [pg. 74]

Nor can we turn a blind eye to those in need, and the evils that hold men and women in addiction and bondage; that would be living in our own little world (and there are too many in the Church doing that already)!

No we must be blind to the things of the world that tantalize the senses. Things that interest our flesh e.g., sex, power, money, and for some even violence.

I've heard it said, **"*Remember, the sin that fascinates you, is the same sin that will assassinate you!*"**

Job said,
> *Job 31:1*
> *I made a covenant with mine eyes; why then should I think upon a maid?*

And John wrote the following.
> *1 John 2:15-17*
> *15. Love not the world, neither the things that are in the world. If any man love the world, the love of the Father is not in him.*
> *16. For all that is in the world, the lust of the flesh, and the lust of the eyes, and the pride of life, is not of the Father, but is of the world.*
> *17. And the world passeth away, and the lust thereof: but he that doeth the will of God abideth for ever.*

The enemy of our souls has no new tricks, the same old temptations and sins he used against people in Bible days, are the same ones he is using against men and women today.

I CAN'T TRUST ME

Our flesh (our carnality) is drawn to those things, that's why they are a temptation to us. The Lord's half-brother James said this about it.

> *James 1:14-16*
> *14. But every man is tempted, when he is drawn away of his own lust, and enticed.*
> *15. Then when lust hath conceived, it bringeth forth sin: and sin, when it is finished, bringeth forth death.*
> *16. Do not err, my beloved brethren.*

The Apostle Paul writing to the Galatians warns; the flesh and the spirit of a man are at odds,[115] or contrary to one another. In laymen's terms: YOUR FLESH FIGHTS YOUR SPIRIT! Pulling the opposite way from what your spirit man knows is right.

> *Galatians 5:19 NIV*
> *The acts of the flesh are obvious: sexual immorality, impurity and debauchery;*

> *Galatians 5:24*
> *And they that are Christ's have crucified the flesh with the affections and lusts.*

And you can't lie to yourself, and say, I know when to stop, or I can handle temptation. If you feel a temptation pulling at you, just stop! **Stop immediately, don't take that next look, don't take that drink, don't stay a moment longer, whatever it is, STOP IT!** Especially in the arena of sexual sins, don't only stop, but run!

---

115   ... these are contrary the one to the other... Gal 5:17 King James Version / Public Domain

1 Corinthians 6:18 NLT
Run from sexual sin! No other sin so clearly affects the body as this one does. For sexual immorality is a sin against your own body.

Don't fight it, don't try to prove how dsciplined you are or how you can endure being tempted; just run from it! Paul told his younger counterpart Timothy how to handle this sort of temptation.

2 Timothy 2:22 NLT
Run from anything that stimulates youthful lusts. Instead, pursue righteous living, faithfulness, love, and peace.

COLD SHOWERS

If you are caught in porn's trap, maybe even caught up in the industry as a worker, actress, actor, model, etc. it may take more than a few cold showers to set you free from its effects. There may be some emotional baggage, physical habits, and spiritual attachments[116] you have picked up that need to be dealt with through Biblical counseling and much fervent prayer.

The devil doesn't want people free, especially if you have been a good customer, so he will try to hold you back. He uses condemnation, cravings, fear, feelings, guilt, images, memories, all to drag you back into what Jesus saved you out of.

Just remember all of Heaven is on your side, and YOU ARE ON THE WINNING TEAM! Pray, pray, pray and read the Bible,

---

116 'spiritual attachments' or soul-ties (n.) A spiritual connection sometimes occurs during interaction between people [often between lovers], animals, even inanimate objects, e.g., a prized possession, keepsakes, memorabilia, etc. can all have a connection either good or bad

study it as if your life depends on it—because it does!

> *James 1:12*
> *Blessed is the man that endureth temptation: for when he is tried, he shall receive the crown of life, which the Lord hath promised to them that love him.*

Join a Bible-believing church and as much as possible stay around other believers who will encourage and pray with you. Ask God to show you each step toward your new bright future in Christ Jesus.

A PRAYER FOR DELIVERANCE

Pray this prayer out loud and bold[117] (declare it with authority.)

> *"Heavenly Father,*
>
> *"I thank You for forgiving me of all my sins. Thank You for giving me freedom through the shed blood of Jesus Christ on the cross. I take my victory He guaranteed when He rose victorious out of the tomb, over all the powers of the enemy.*
>
> *"Now I stand in that victory and use the authority He gave me as one of His followers to take back my life. I have been delivered from Satan's kingdom and the powers of darkness and translated over into the Kingdom of Jesus, Your only Son! I AM FREE! The Son has set me free and I am now free indeed! I AM FREE!*
>
> *"Satan I bind you and every one of your little minions and*

---

117   ... but the righteous are bold as a lion. Proverbs 28:1b King James Version / Public Domain

imps that would even think to come against me; you are hereby given notice to cease any and all operations against me now in Jesus' Name! I AM FREE! All spirits of darkness, all spirits of lust, pornography or immorality, and any demonic forces operating for or within the porn industry, you are immediately released from any assignments against me in Jesus' Name! I AM FREE! I will not be hindered by any fear, habit, memory, demon, entity, fallen angel, or seducing spirit, not now, NOT EVER! All attachments, curses, enchantments, habits, hooks, soul-ties and spells are broken now in Jesus' Name! I AM FREE!

"The blood of Jesus cleanses me from all sins, and no weapon formed against me prospers. I am a child of God! Thank you Lord for setting me free! I AM FREE in Jesus' Name Amen!"

LIFE IN THE WORD

Galatians 5:16
This I say then, Walk in the Spirit, and ye shall not fulfil the lust of the flesh.

Now as a Christian man or woman get in The Word of God, read it, study it; dig into The Bible like a man searching for buried treasure. Recognize this is God talking to mankind, speaking to you in written form. **Spending time in your Bible is the number one way to get to know God, it's the number one way to stay clear of Satan's traps; it's your roadmap to success as a Believer.**

Look at the following verses about the life-changing power found in The Bible.

Proverbs 25:2
It is the glory of God to conceal a thing: but the honour of kings is to <u>search out</u> a matter.

Psalms 107:20
He sent <u>his word</u>, and healed them, and delivered them from their destructions.

Romans 10:17
So then faith cometh by hearing, and hearing <u>by the word</u> of God.

Ephesians 5:26 NLT
to make her[118] holy and clean, washed by the cleansing of God's word.

2 Timothy 2:15
Study to shew thyself approved unto God, a workman that needeth not to be ashamed, rightly dividing the word of truth.

And Paul wrote to the Romans,
Romans 12:2
And be not conformed to this world: but be ye transformed by <u>the renewing of your mind</u>, that ye may prove what is that good, and acceptable, and perfect, will of God.

That renewing of the mind only comes by studying your Bible and prayer time, (talking to God and listening for His instruction). For you're building a relationship with Him. He set you free, now trust Him to keep you and lead you by His Spirit into all truth.

---

118   'her' as a pronoun speaking of or referring to the Church

Their feet run to evil, and they make haste to shed innocent blood:
their thoughts are thoughts of iniquity;
wasting and destruction are in their paths.
Isaiah 59:7

Epilogue

Chris' Story

Growing up I always enjoyed going to my grandmother's house, I was spoiled in her love in a way only a grandparent could do. As I reflect back on my earlier years, I don't seem to have many memories of not being at her house, but there was a dark side to staying there. My uncle was a porn addict, whose addiction was no longer satisfied with only watching, it turned into action against a young child; against me.

I would have to guess I was around 4 to 5 years of age when it happened for the first time. He called me into his room and began to sexually abuse me. Scared, I never yelled or fought back. This went on for a few years, until my family moved from Maryland to West Virginia. But by that point in time I must have been raped well over 80 times. I thought I was now safe, but I was confused, hurt and still scared. I remember coming home from school that year for Christmas break, and when I walked into my room my grandmother was sitting on my bed, arms wide open. Being a grandma's boy, I ran straight into her arms, clinging to her with so much joy from missing her tender love and affection. But when the excitement ended, I saw to my left my uncle, the past was back to torment me more.

At this point I would say that I was more ashamed than afraid of what was happening. During this time while everyone else was enjoying the company of one another, I was hurting and putting on a mask to hide what was right in front of everyone else. Yet again my uncle found a way to get me alone and continued his desire of lust. Christmas came to an end and I prayed for a freedom for myself from this man as well, as he drove back with my grandmother to Maryland. At this point I believe I was in 3rd grade. I was now fully aware of what was happening between he and I, but I was also aware of the fact this man took care of my grandmother who otherwise could not have made it on her own, so I kept quiet.

We soon after moved to West Virginia to a small town called Summersville. I loved being in school, as long as I was in school, I knew it was safe. I hated thanksgiving break, Christmas break and Summer and Spring, there was always a chance of running into my uncle and becoming his personal toy. When I was 14 he came down to West Virginia once again during thanksgiving break, at this point I was messed up sexually, I did not know if I was gay or straight, I began to blame myself for what happened and that somehow, I deserved it. But when he came into my room this time I looked him right into the eyes and said "NO!". That was the last time he attempted to touch me, but I still kept a mask for years, not wanting to break my grandmother's heart from knowing the truth about her son.

In High School, I became addicted to porn. If there was a girl willing, I would go for her and if she was not, I would use every trick I knew to charm her into sex. At the end of my high school career I hated myself for what I had done, what I was becoming. It was at that moment I realized that porn was the starting ground, the gateway to what fed the lust in my uncle and now in me. I knew he watched it as I saw it on his computer many times while he abused me, but it did not click until this moment. I started going back to church and asked my youth leader for help, sadly I hit a brick wall. I returned to porn and the lust with it. I left the church out of anger, feeling that no one really wanted to help someone in need, that no one wanted to help me. So, I went back to parties, throwing a few of my own and sleeping with any girl who would say yes. I thank God that He corrects those He loves and convicts us of sin.

~

> *To the person struggling with porn and lust, know it will never fill the void you are attempting to fill. It will lead you down a path of destruction.*

Everyone knew me as "preacher boy" in elementary, middle and high school. I always had a Bible and preached to anyone I could in the classroom, the playground or the bus. But that died down in about 11th grade, shortly after becoming a certified biblical life coach. I was at a party with some old friends from high school and as the party progressed, I got more drunk and more into the flesh, dancing, smoking and making out with several girls, when out of nowhere I heard a voice yell out, "Is that preacher boy?!". When I heard this my drink fell straight out of my hands and I began to weep uncontrollably. I turned to see an old acquaintance who I never got along with because of my beliefs and his party hard lifestyle conflicting, he came up to me and asked, "What happened, I thought you were different from us?" I ran out like a bullet from a barrel, weeping the whole way home.

I remember going to my porn stash (it was paper as I did not have a phone with internet or a computer) and ran to the bathroom, shredded the paper and flushed it away. I later talked to my friends and asked them to forgive me for not walking out what I used to preach to them in school. I also repented to God and asked Him to help me, to show me the way to overcome this addiction. I eventually found my way to a church that had a genuine care for people and they brought me into the revelation of the ministry of the Holy Ghost, a teaching that was frowned upon in the church I had left prior.

I came to learn the truth about my addiction and the abuse, as both the pastor of this church and Holy Ghost ministered to me. I came to see that porn and sex were nothing more than a substitute for the genuine love of my Father. If I could say anything to The Church, it would be; not to judge or hold porn addiction to some different standard than any other addiction, but to help those who need it, with the same care as they would any other addiction. At least in my case, I was so afraid of the shame I feared telling anyone, I felt I had no safe place to go. To the person struggling with porn and lust, know it will never fill the void you are attempting to fill. It will lead you down a path of destruction. It may feel good, but it will never give you fulfilment.

After all of this happened, I still had to overcome my abuser. One day on my way to work, I saw my stepmother getting in her car. It took me off guard due to the fact that she was normally at work by this time and she was not wearing the attire for her job. I went to her car and asked her what she was doing. She responded, "I'm going to pick up your uncle." My gut sank and I felt like hurling, it had been a few months from the last time I saw him at my sister's wedding. This time I could not put the everything-is-ok mask back on. I told my stepmother the truth about what her brother did. It fell on deaf ears. I went to stay at my boss Jennifer's house, a woman I now call mother. I called that night, begging my family to send my uncle back home. They did and I came back the next day. When I talked to my father and mother I was all but called a liar, I was told my grandmother did not want to see me and that I was not welcome back in Maryland. As deep as that cut me and brought pain, I had at least let the truth be told.

To this day, I am sure my family still does not believe what I told them. After all it is a hard pill to swallow, it's hard to accept the truth and knowing that the whole time your son was being sexually abused you did nothing about it. I have, through the grace of God reached out to my uncle and let him know I forgave him for what he did to me and that I hope he will come to be overwhelmed by the love of God.

Finally brothers, whatever is true, whatever is honorable,
whatever is just, whatever is pure, whatever is lovely,
whatever is commendable — if there is any moral excellence
and if there is any praise — dwell on these things.
Philippians 4:8 HCSB

Conclusion

You are FREE!

I pray you have been informed, shocked, appalled, awakened, repentant, forgiven, encouraged and now determined about the porn industry. **<u>Determined</u> to turn from it, reject it and pray for others who are still caught in it.**

I know that with God's help, you can do this. I DECLARE IT! If you have been set free through the teaching and the prayers in this book, **YOU WILL REMAIN FREE IN JESUS' NAME!**

1 Corinthians 10:13
There hath no temptation taken you but such as is common
to man: but God is faithful, who will not suffer you to be
tempted above that ye are able; but will with the temptation
also make a way to escape, that ye may be able to bear it.

If you are tempted, don't look at it, LOOK UP! Set your sights on Heaven and decide to live for Jesus every day. Don't look back, this old world has nothing to offer. **Jesus has given you new life; sin has no hold on your life. YOU ARE FREE! <u>You have overcome in Jesus' Name!</u> I DECLARE YOU WILL NEVER GO BACK!**

Bibliography

I consulted the following works while researching and writing this book. This is not a complete list of resources on this topic, and I encourage you to do your own research to find the latest information on this topic. Please do not use this list as a model for the format of your own book or report.

1. Encyclopedia Britannica
2. www.ancient-wisdom.co.uk
3. Wikipedia [History of erotic depictions]
4. Ilan Ben Zion, Israel Museum, timesofisrael.com
5. Many historians, e.g., John Keay approximate likely 200 CE
6. debauchery' Sodomy [is generally anal or oral sex between people] Wikipedia 1/20/17
7. Wikipedia/https://en.wikipedia.org/w/index.php?title =Fanny_Hill&oldid=771125680
8. Pravda.ru [History of pornography: scandalous beginning and habitual reality] - 11/27/2007
9. The Accessible Archives; Britannica.com / https://www.britannica.com/event/Comstock-Act / Published: December 01, 1999 - Accessed 04/2016
10. pornographyhistory.com and various online information sources / Dec 2015
11. "taboo" prohibited or restricted by social custom: adj. / Oxford Dictionaries / Yahoo
12. Google.com, pornographyhistory.com
13. Wikipedia contributors. "Hugh Hefner." Wikipedia, The Free Encyclopedia.
14. Playboy -- American monthly magazine for men [The Editors of Encyclopædia Britannica] Encyclopædia Britannica, inc / http://www. britannica.com/topic/Playboy

15. Penthouse men's magazine / owned by Global Media Inc / Wikipedia The Free Encyclopedia / https://en.wikipedia.org/w/index.php?title=Penthouse_(magazine)&oldid=768610036

16. Hustler adult magazine / Wikipedia, The Free Encyclopedia. / https://en.wikipedia.org/w/index.php?title=Pornographic_magazine&oldid=764525911

17. history.com Marilyn Monroe is found dead / http://www.history.com/this-day-in-history/marilyn-monroe-is-found-dead

18. "Roth v. United States." Oyez, https://www.oyez.org/cases/1956/582.

19. "I am Curious (Yellow); Whitebloom, Kenny (10 August 2011). "The Curious Case of 'I am Curious'". Boston TV News Digital Library

20. "Moral Dilemmas" J. Kerby Anderson (1989)

21. Wikipedia contributors "William Bill Rotsler" The free encyclopedia. Accessed 2016

22. "California vs. Freeman": [The revenge of the Magic Camera] theintenttoarouse.com

23. "© 2015 Covenant Eyes. All rights reserved. Originally published at CovenantEyes.com."

24. "The Stats on Internet Pornography" by Tim (2013) dailyinfographic.com

25. http://www.familysafemedia.com

26. familysafemedia.com

27. "The Numbers Behind Pornography" by Stewart Cowan (2013) dailyinfographic.com

28. (Lifestyle Trends) / chinadaily.com

29. dailyinfographic.com, crosswalk.com

30. CP Living at Christianpost.com

31. Ezekiel 3:17, 33:7

32. Numbers 32:23

33. Then they brought the golden vessels that were taken out of

the temple of the house of God... Dan 5:1-5 King James Version /
Public Domain

34. Genesis 8:22

35. Galatians 6:8

36. 'Kingdom of Light II kingdom of Darkness -- Spiritual Warfare and The Church' by Minister Michael R. Hicks (2017) Used
by permission.

37. ... there is no truth in him (John 8:44)

38. "Voyeur." Merriam-Webster.com. Merriam-Webster, n.d. Web.
7 Jan. 2016.

39. clinicalcareconsultants.com, by Dr. Maryanne Layden [Por-
nography Statistics]

40. Paper to the Surgeon General's Workshop on Pornography
and Public Health, University of Indiana: -- Alington, Virginia
(June 1986)

41. (*Described as the world's leading anti-pornography campaigner)
from [Pornland: How Porn has Hijacked our Sexuality] 04/26/2011
Beacon Press

42. Paper to the Surgeon General's Workshop on Pornography
and Public Health, University of Indiana: -- Alington, Virginia
(June 1986)

43. U.S. Congress Permanent Subcommittee on Investigations
on Child Pornography and Pedophilia (1986)

44. US Department of Justice [Research on Pornography] documented antisex.com

45. from "Moral Dilemmas" by J. Kerby Anderson (1998)

46. statisticbrain.com [Accessed 2015]

47. Lt. Darrell H. Pope [Research on Pornography] - antisex.com

48. dosomething.org

49. Romans 12:15 / http://www.BlueLetterBible.org / Accessed
2017.

50. 'blush' New Strong's Exhaustive Concordance [by James

Strong] May 21, 2003

51. 'gross' New Strong's Exhaustive Concordance [James Strong] May 21, 2003

52. 'wax cold' ψύχω (psü'-khō) New Strong's Exhaustive Concordance [by James Strong] May 21, 2003

53. 'keep' New Strong's Exhaustive Concordance [by James Strong] May 21, 2003

54. the thief cometh but to kill, steal and to destroy. John 10:10

55. 1 Timothy 3:7; 2 Timothy 2:26

56. 2 Timothy 2:3

57. ...an angel of light 2 Corinthians 11:14

58. ...for they know his voice. John 10:4

59. the Moberly Monitor-Index in Missouri reporting

60. According to The New York Times

61. May 1959 the Associated Press (AP) noted

62. "Bikini" Encyclopædia Britannica by The Editors of Encyclopædia Britannica / Published May 15, 2015 / https://www.britannica.com/place/Bikini-atoll-Marshall-Islands

63. Flee also youthful lusts. 2 Timothy 2:22

64. 'EVERY MAN'S BATTLE - Winning the War on Sexual Temptation One Victory at a Time' by Stephen Arterburn and Fred Stoeker / The Crown Publishing Group / 01/20/2004

65. Bondi 'Bikini Wars' – Arrests on Sydney Beaches (1940s – 1960s) / http://www.xploresydney.com

66. Sports Illustrated / Brendan Ripp / New York, USA / http://www.SI.com

67. Cosmopolitan / Hearst / http://www.cosmopolitan.com

68. Esquire / Hearst Companies / New York, New York USA / http://www.esquire.com

69. Hooters / Atlanta, GA. / http://www.hooters.com

70. Twin Peaks [Restaurant franchise] Addison, Tx. / http://www.twinpeaksrestaurant.com / Wikipedia, The Free Encyclopedia, 17

Jan. 2017 Accessed 03/08/17

71. Tilted Kilt / founded in Las Vegas, Nevada / Headquarters: Tempe, AZ. / http://www.tiltedkilt.com / http://illuminatimind-control.com/breastaurant-hottest-trend-casual-dining/

72. Brickhouse Tavern / Ignite Restaurant Group / Houston TX 77042 / brickhousetavernandtap.com

73. ... a discerner of the thoughts and intents of the heart. Hebrews 4:12 / King James Version

74. goodreads.com "Martin Luther"

75. Live joyfully with the wife whom thou lovest ... Ecclesiastes 9:9 / Marriage is honourable in all, and the bed undefiled ... Hebrews 13:4 King James Version / Public Domain

76. ... the body is not for fornication / Flee fornication... 1 Corinthians 6:14, 18

77. muumuu [mu:mu:] is a loose dress of Hawaiian origin that hangs from the shoulder. / Wikipedia, The Free Encyclopedia. Accessed 3/09/17

78. rut - the periodically recurring sexual excitement of the deer, goat, sheep, etc. / Dictionary.com. Dictionary.com Unabridged. Random House, Inc. http://www.dictionary.com/browse/rut

79. Rev. Creflo Dollar described 'lust' as a desire that could not be lawfully fulfilled.

80. Many of the references used in this segue '4 KINDS OF LOVE' were retrieved from The Blue Letter Bible online / http://www.blueletterbible.org / Accessed 2015

81. agapē [the love of God] wikipedia.com

82. phileō / http://www.biblestudytools.com

83. storgē / http://www.truthortradition.com

84. Be kindly affectioned one to another with brotherly love... Romans 12:10a

85. Genesis 10:19 'Sodom' A city of ancient Palestine possibly located south of the Dead Sea. (n.d.) American Heritage®

Dictionary of the English Language, Fifth Edition. (2011). http://www.thefreedictionary.com/Sodom

86. Genesis 6:17 [flood of Noah] approximately 4,359 years ago in the year 1656 AM or 2348 BC / David Wright, AiG–U.S. / http://www.answersingenesis.org

87. "we may know them" [to know (a person carnally] Source: Blue Letter Bible online / http://www.blueletterbible.org

88. For he shall give his angels charge over thee... Psalms 91:11; Luke 4:10

89. The thief cometh not, but for to steal, and to kill, and to destroy... John 10:10 / King James Version

90. 'Covenant' a divine promise establishing or modifying God's relationship to humanity / (n.d.) American Heritage® Dictionary of the English Language, Fifth Edition. (2011). Retrieved March 10 2017 from http://www.thefreedictionary.com

91. 'tokens' a blood-stained sheet or cloth from the bed where a marriage is consummated. The blood (dam betulim) is said to "prove" the bride's virginity... / Peter C. Craigie, The Book of Deuteronomy (NICOT; Grand Rapids: Eerdmans, 1976), 292-293 [online] http://hermeneutics.stackexchange.com/questions

92. a fold of mucous membrane partly closing the external orifice of the vagina in a virgin. / hymen. (n.d.). Dictionary.com Unabridged. Retrieved March 13, 2017

93. 'betrothed' to join or marry; the King James Version uses the word 'espoused' / Source: Blue Letter Bible online / http://www.blueletterbible.org

94. Focus on the Family online / The Impact of Pornography on Marital Sex by Juli Slattery http://www.focusonthefamily.com/marriage/sex-and-intimacy/when-your-husband-isnt-interested-in-sex/the-impact-of-pornography-on-marital-sex

95. "normalcy" the state of being normal. / Random House Kernerman Webster's College Dictionary, © 2010 K Dictionaries

Ltd. Copyright 2005, 1997, 1991 by Random House, Inc. All rights reserved.

96. Cline, Pornography's Effects, 3-5. iiVictor B. Cline, "Pornography and Sexual Addictions," Christian Counseling Today 4, no. 4 (1996): 58. https://www.protectkids.com/effects/patternofaddiction.htm

97. Hebrews 13:4 King James Version / Public domain

98. The Message Bible © 2002 by Eugene H. Peterson / Bible Gateway online / https://www.biblegateway.com

99. Some references retrieved from the La Vista Church of Christ website. Used by Permission. http://lavistachurchofchrist.org/LVanswers/2006/11-02.htm

100. ... enjoy the pleasures of sin for a season; Hebrews 11:25b King James Version

101. Jesus saith unto him, I am the way, the truth, and the life: no man cometh unto the Father, but by me. John 14:6 / Source: Blue Letter Bible online / http://www.blueletterbible.org

102, 103. 'conversion' a turning to embrace God / Elwell, Walter A. "Entry for 'Convert, Conversion'". "Evangelical Dictionary of Theology". . 1997.

104. 'Rahab the harlot' Joshua 6:17 King James Version / Public domain

105. 'King David's affair' 2 Samuel 11:2-27, 12:13, 24 King James Version / Public Domain / Blue Letter Bible online / http://www.blueletterbible.org

106. 'Gomer' Hosea 3:1-3 King James Bible / Public domain

107. 'Mary Magdalene' the woman from whom He had cast out seven demons. Mk 16:9 NLT

108. 'madman of the Gadarenes' Luke 8:26-36 King James Version / Public domain

109. 'woman taken in adultery' John 8:3-11 King James version / Public Domain

110. All of "The Roman Road to Salvation" verses taken from the New Living Translation of the Bible / For everyone has sinned we." Blue Letter Bible. Web. 16 Mar, 2017. <https://www.blueletterbible.org/nlt/rom/3/23/s_1049023>.

111. Dating Paul's letter to the Romans (A.D. 56-58); then writing his 2nd letter to the Corinthian Church between (A.D. 55-57)

112. Keep thy heart with all diligence; for out of it are the issues of life. Pro 4:23 King James Version / Public Domain

113. Lest Satan should get an advantage of us: for we are not ignorant of his devices. 2 Co 2:11 King James Version / Public Domain

114. agapē - refers to the love of God love that motivates to demonstrative action SEE: Ch. 8 'Making Love' segue '4 KINDS OF LOVE' [pg. 74]

115. ... these are contrary the one to the other... Gal 5:17 King James Version / Public Domain

116. 'spiritual attachments' or soul-ties (n.) A spiritual connection sometimes occurs during interaction between people [often between lovers], animals, even inanimate objects, e.g., a prized possession, keepsakes, memorabilia, etc. can all have a connection either good or bad

117. ... but the righteous are bold as a lion. Proverbs 28:1b King James Version / Public Domain

118. 'her' as a pronoun speaking of or referring to the Church

About the Author

Aaron Jones is the founder of Aaron Jones Global Net Ministry and a missionary to the nations.

With a special love for God's Leaders: The Apostles, Prophets, Evangelists, Pastors, and Teachers (often referred to as the Fivefold Ministry), Aaron speaks in Leadership and Pastors Conferences around the world. His focus is on igniting a divine fire in these leaders, and then building and assisting them in their Churches, Businesses and even in Government positions to effectively finish the task God has called each individual to do.

The Spirit of God spoke direct orders to Aaron one night at Rhema Bible Church in Broken Arrow, Oklahoma,
   "Go to the nations and ignite my leaders with the fire of the Holy Ghost; and people will gather from miles around to watch them burn, and they will ignite others for my Kingdom."

To accomplish this, Aaron will continue to go forth and send others into the high places and the low places of the world, in search of those God has called to accomplish great things.

Aaron says,
   "By connecting the life-changing power of God's Word with the gifts and talents He has placed in each individual, we are raising up successful Christian Leaders around the globe.

   "Greatness is already in these Men and Women of God. The Holy Spirit did that, when they were created. Many times they just need someone to see it, and pull it out of them."

In 2015 he established 'The Greater Tulsa Area Ministers and Missionaries Breakfast Fellowship' - a monthly meeting designed to promote unity within the denominations and ministries in and around Tulsa, Oklahoma. Then corporately pray for our nation, and help promote missions and evangelism.

He is an accomplished professional Illustrator, Wildlife Artist and the Author of six books:

● **In the SECRET PLACE of the MOST HIGH**
God's Word for Supernatural Healing, Deliverance & Protection

● **SOUND from HEAVEN**
Praying in Tongues for a Victorious Life

● **People of the PROMISE**

● **The Confessions of a Victorious Believer**
Speaking GOD'S WORD into your life

● **Lace, Lust & LIES**
Our shameful affair with the Porn Industry

● **FIVE SMOOTH STONES**

He currently resides with his family just outside of Tulsa, Oklahoma and is available for Meetings, Conferences and Revivals.

Contact at:
boldtruthbooks@yahoo.com

Check out these other Great Books from
BOLD TRUTH PUBLISHING

-----

by Judy Spencer
• TURN OFF THE STEW

-----

by Ronnie Moore
• THE BLOOD COVENANT

-----

by Wayne W. Sanders
• EFFECTIVE PRISON Ministries

------

by Daryl P Holloman
• Seemed Good to The Holy Ghost
Five Anointed Teachings by Brother Daryl
PLUS - Prayers, Prophecy, Testimonies and more ...

-----

by B. Steve Young
• SIX FEET DEEP
Burying Your Past with Forgiveness

-----

by Jerry W. Hollenbeck
• The KINGDOM of GOD
An Agrarian Society

-----

by Aaron Jones
• The CONFESSIONS of a VICTORIOUS BELIEVER
Speaking GOD'S WORD into your life

-----

by Ed Marr
• C. H. P. - Coffee Has Priority
The Memoirs of a California Highway Patrol Officer
Badge 9045

by Mary Ann England
• Women in Ministry
From her Teachings at FCF Bible School - Tulsa, OK.
(Foreword by Pat Harrison)

------

by Michael R. Hicks
• KINGDOM of LIGHT II - kingdom of darkness
Spiritual Warfare and The Church

------

by Elizabeth Pruitt Sloan
• The Holy Spirit SPEAKS Expressly

------

by Rick McKnight
• Matthew 4:4
Man shall not live by bread alone,
but by every word that proceedeth out of the mouth of God.

-----

by Rachel V. Jeffries
• PITIFUL or POWERFUL?
THE CHOICE IS YOURS

-----

by Jean Carlburg
• I Have a Story to Tell
He that believeth on me, as the scripture hath said,
out of his belly shall flow rivers of living water. - John 7:38

------

by Lynn Whitlock Jones
• SPIRITUAL BIRTHING
Bringing God's Plans & Purposes into Manifestation

See more Books and all of our products at
www.BoldTruthPublishing.com

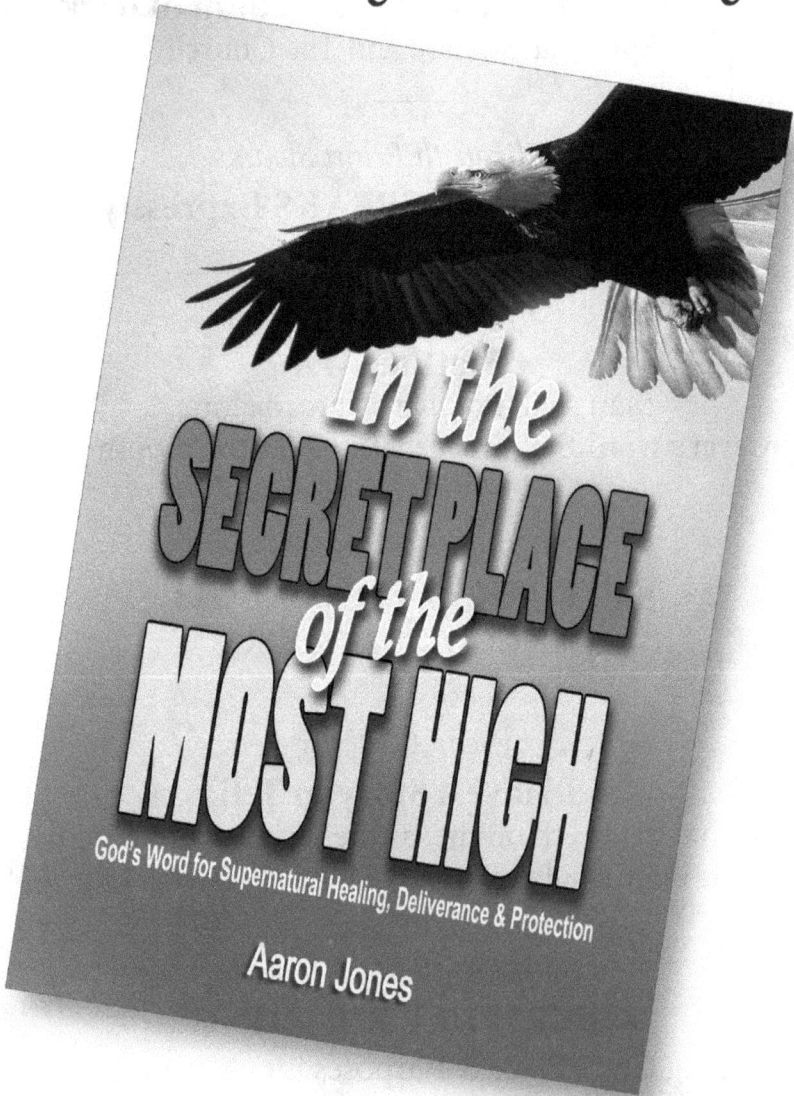

www.ingramcontent.com/pod-product-compliance
Lightning Source LLC
Chambersburg PA
CBHW072153270326
41930CB00011B/2409